Marshal Villars

and the War of the
Spanish Succession

CLAUDE C. STURGILL

Marshal Villars
and the War of the Spanish Succession

UNIVERSITY *of* KENTUCKY PRESS

TO

S. T. McCloy

Preface

THIS STUDY IS FOCUSED ON ONE INDIVIDUAL—MARSHAL Claude Villars—but behind him stood the entire military organization of France, and of its structure in the seventeenth and eighteenth centuries we know very little. We may be reasonably sure of answers to our questions from the time of Napoleon onwards and before the time of Louis XIV. But in between lies a period of one hundred and fifty years. During this period the emphasis of historians has been on the social and cultural fields to the neglect of the development of French military institutions. Perhaps one day a series of studies will appear that will not only discuss the civil-military relationship and the evolution of tactical systems in France but will also determine the levels of French military achievement in the various arms and functions—the final basis of authority in any state system—as these existed along the road that led eventually to Napoleon.

The entire resources of the powerful kingdom of France were mobilized and used throughout the period 1661-1715 to obtain the territorial wishes of Louis XIV. It must have been clear to Louis in 1665 that he was entering a period of long and exhausting warfare. One war was to follow another as he found that the powers of Europe were determined to prevent French domination of Europe, just as in times past they had opposed the possibility of Habsburg domination.

The concept of the balance of power forbade that any one nation or combination of states should become strong enough to exert continental or colonial superiority.

Although Louis insisted that he had been victorious in the War of Devolution (1667-1668), the Dutch War (1676-1678), and the War of the League of Augsburg (1688-1697), it was apparent that the growing strength of the Emperor and the increasing opposition of Protestatn Europe would compel him to focus his attention on the possessions of Spain, in fact upon the Spanish crown itself. Louis' last war, that of the Spanish Succession (1701-1714), which was to embrace not only Europe but the colonial possessions of the contending powers in the Americas and the Far East, was the result of his losses in the north. That this policy of almost continuous war footing and national exhaustion did not lead France to utter ruin and partition during the War of the Spanish Succession was due in no small measure to the talents of Marshal Claude Villars.

The present study has attempted to place Marshal Villars in his proper place in the military history of France. Possibly others have let this opportunity go by because of haste, lack of proper training, or failure to study the archival materials. I have tried to steer a middle course between his two principal biographers, the Duke of Saint-Simon and Lieutenant Colonel Carré. Villars is presented not as a self-seeking Machiavellian character (Saint-Simon) nor as the last of the great French knights (Carré). He stands out so significantly because he was greatly superior in ability to the other French marshals during the War of the Sapnish Succession.

Villars entered the French army at the age of seventeen in the grade of second lieutenant. Save for brief intervals he spent his entire adult life on the field of campaign. By 1697 Villars had risen to the rank of lieutenant general, despite grave handicaps of birth and family, in a time when the sons of many noble families began their military careers with a rank of at least lieutenant colonel. He had experienced the terror and joy of battle and had obtained that understanding of the common soldier that comes only after long years of close association.

With the opening of the War of the Spanish Succession Villars was in his proper element. After an extremely frustrating experience as second-in-command to Marshal Catinat (1701-1702) he was given a separate command and ordered to march to the aid of the Elector of Bavaria. The defeat of the Prince of Baden at Friedlingen (October 1702) brought Villars promotion to Marshal of France. The Count of Styrum met a similar defeat at Höchstädt in 1703. Serious arguments with the Elector of Bavaria over the conduct of the war forced Louis XIV to recall Villars in disgrace. By suppression of the Camisard Revolt in 1704 he regained the king's favor. From 1705 to 1708 Villars acted as a fireman— holding the Rhine (1705-1707) and Alpine (1708) frontiers while other generals made major efforts on the Flanders front. The consequences of a series of defeats in Flanders at the hands of the Duke of Marlborough and Prince Eugene plus the terrible winter of 1708-1709 prompted Louis XIV to give Villars command in Flanders in early 1709. Villars instilled sufficient martial spirit in the hungry, crumbling Army of Flanders to achieve a bloody but decisive draw at Malplaquet. Although partially crippled and in intense pain from a knee cap shattered in that battle Villars led the defense of northern France during the years of attrition (1710-1711). The success of Louis XIV in detaching the English from the Grand Alliance in early 1712 led to Villars' victory at Denain. A final successful campaign on the Rhine against Eugene (1713) saw Landau and Freiburg become French. Villars received the distinct honor of negotiating the Treaty of Rastat (March 7, 1714) which ended the War of the Spanish Succession.

Villars was a general whose only tactic was to fight the enemy wherever and whenever possible. He is best described by the words loyal, courageous, conceited, defiant, impulsive, arrogant, uncooperative, and resourceful. Others have said that Villars was the savior of France. I seriously doubt that Villars was a great military tactician, on a par even with Gustavus Adolphus or Marshal Saxe, but certainly France would have lost far more in the War of the Spanish Succession without him.

Whatever merits this book may display are due in great measure to the talents and efforts of Dr. Shelby T. McCloy and to the helpful suggestions of Drs. Thomas D. Clark, Carl B. Cone, Thomas C. Walker of the University of Kentucky and of Dr. Enno E. Kraehe of the University of North Carolina at Chapel Hill.

Many have criticized European officialdom for a cool, aloof attitude. I can accord only praise of the highest order to numerous French and Austrian officials who aided my researches in European archives. In fact, these officials not only showed willingness to be of assistance but in many cases seemed to fear that I might not be getting enough help. Space will not permit me to acknowledge their help individually.

To all the above individuals and institutions I express my appreciation. The mistakes are mine.

Oshkosh, Wisconsin   C. C .S.
January, 1965

Contents

CHAPTER ONE

The White Coat of France

IN THE GRAND COURTYARD OF THE PALACE OF VERSAILLES
there is an equestrian statue of Louis XIV, inscribed "King,
by the Grace of God, of all France and Navarre." On sunny
days the raised right arm of the statue, which holds the
fleur-de-lis of a marshal of France, casts a long shadow towards
the Rhine frontier. This statue symbolizes the reason why
Louis XIV was a threat to the European balance of power.
Louis' desire to extend the French frontiers to what he
believed to be their natural boundaries—the Alps, the Rhine
and the Pyrenees—inaugurated, in 1661, a period of fifty-
three years during which he would attempt to make France
the dominant European power. To some contemporaries
success might have seemed only a matter of a few months
when, on November 1, 1700, Charles II of Spain died and
Louis XIV's grandson, Philip of Anjou, was declared the
heir designate to all the vast possessions of the Spanish
inheritance. Actually this royal death merely completed a
chain of events during the reign of Louis XIV which set
the stage for the War of the Spanish Succession.

The major cause of this fourth and last war of Louis XIV
lies in the political-military history of the Kingdom of France.

Although the Peace of Westphalia (1648) and the Peace of the Pyrenees (1659) had extinguished the last reasonable hopes of the Habsburgs for European domination, these treaties had not settled the problem that France, from the early sixteenth century, had set out to resolve. France still feared Habsburg encirclement. Any map of western Europe for the midseventeenth century will show that Lille, Besançon, the Two Sicilies, and Milan were still in the hands of the Spanish branch of the Habsburgs. A further glance at the map convinces one that the Austrian Habsburgs were still a power to be reckoned with. There still existed the possibility that the Habsburgs of Spain and of the Holy Roman Empire might reunite. Should this happen, the Habsburg power might still encircle France. Consequently, when Mazarin died in 1661 and Louis XIV, at the age of twenty-three, assumed full powers, the century-old problem of destroying the Habsburg ring became his political inheritance.

Louis' first opportunity for action came with the death of his wife's father, Philip IV of Spain, in 1665. It will be recalled that upon her marriage to Louis XIV Maria Theresa had renounced all her claims to the Spanish inheritance, with the stipulation that France would receive a large dowry of gold bullion. This portion of the marriage contract had not been carried out. In 1665 Louis used this forfeiture and the ambiguous Law of Devolution that existed in several of the provinces of the Spanish Netherlands to lay claim to that entire portion of the map known as the Spanish Netherlands.

The entire resources of the powerful kingdom of France were mobilized and used throughout the period 1661-1715 to obtain the territorial wishes of Louis XIV. These involved extension of the French frontier to the Rhine and to the Scheldt at the expense of the Habsburgs and usurpation of the Emperor's position as the temporal leader of the Catholic Church. Therefore it could not have been anything less than abundantly clear to Louis XIV in 1665 that he was entering upon a period of long and exhausting warfare. But little did this "greatest of the Bourbons" dream that his desires would place his royal house firmly upon the road to revolution and ruin.

Thus one war was to follow another as Louis found that the powers of Europe were equally determined that French domination of Europe should not come about, just as in times past they had opposed the possibility of Habsburg domination. The concept of the balance of power forbade that any one nation or combination of states should become strong enough to exert continental or colonial superiority. At first the powerful military machine of France was successful. In the War of Devolution (1667-1668) French arms secured a series of towns and fortresses in the Spanish Netherlands. But in the Dutch War (1676-1678) Louis XIV faced the first of a series of European coalitions when the Holy Roman Empire, Spain, Sweden, and Denmark came to the aid of the United Provinces. Even here Louis continued to show gains; Spain ceded Franche-Comté and another string of fortresses in the Spanish Netherlands. A third war, that of the League of Augsburg (1688-1697), came as a result of Louis' attempts to add further German territories to his realm. Louis found the Emperor Leopold and William of Orange (king of England from 1689) allied as the principals in an anti-French league that carried the war into Asia and North America. By the Peace of Ryswick, which ended this third war, Louis lost some of his fortresses in the Spanish Netherlands, gained some commercial concessions from the Dutch, and was forced to recognize William of Orange as the legitimate king of England. Although Louis insisted that he had been victorious in all three wars, it was clear that the growing strength of the emperor and the increasing opposition of Protestant Europe would compel him to focus his attention on the possessions of Spain, in fact upon the Spanish crown itself. Out of his losses to the north and east was to come Louis' last war, that of the Spanish Succession (1701-1714), which was to embrace not only Europe but the colonial possessions of the contending powers in the Americas and the Far East.

But not only were national interests at stake; after the revocation of the Edict of Nantes in 1685 Louis XIV was the sworn enemy of most Protestants, who saw their liberties imperiled. The wave of religious persecution in France and Louis XIV's support of the dethroned House of Stuart after 1688 aroused European opinion against France as never before. Anglican England and the Calvinist United Provinces had an additional reason to resist further French expansion in Europe and in the colonial sphere.

After having lived some forty years longer than the most optimistic physician thought possible, the tragically deformed, sickly, impotent Charles II of Spain finally died in 1700 without a direct heir. All Europe was interested in the disposition of a patrimony that included Spain and her vast possessions in the New World, in Italy, and in the Low Countries. Louis XIV and the Emperor Leopold I were possible heirs. The United Provinces pondered the fate of the Spanish Netherlands and England coveted the Spanish colonies. Both Louis XIV and the Holy Roman Emperor had dynastic claims to this vast inheritance, but political considerations were to outweigh those of a more legalistic nature. The assumption of the Spanish throne by an Austrian or a French prince would reverse the revered balance of power in Europe and undoubtedly provoke a general war. To avoid this war Louis XIV in 1697 had proposed to William III of England and the Holy Roman Emperor a compact which would divide the possessions of Charles II in an equitable manner and which would ensure the continued tranquility of Europe.

Several projects of partition were discussed. Finally in

1700 England and the United Provinces were able to agree with France on two points. The Spanish crown would be assumed by the cadet branch of the Austrian Habsburgs on the stipulation that Spain and Austria would never be united under the same crown or king. France was to receive Spain's Italian possessions, with the liberty of exchanging them for Lorraine, Luxemburg, Nice, and Savoy.

But, before the partition could take place, it was necessary to gain the agreement of the Habsburg Emperor. William and the Grand Pensionary of Holland, Heinsius, were charged with gaining the consent of their ally, the Emperor Leopold. They approached him with such mild diplomacy that Leopold refused his signature. Neither England nor Holland wished to ratify the treaty without the assurance of Habsburg military support. France could not be sure that she would receive the promised territories, and her important sacrifice of the Spanish throne had created an impression of weakness throughout Europe in regard to her military establishments. London, Vienna, Paris, and The Hague were all sure that Charles II of Spain had made a will which left his possessions to the Austrian Archduke Charles.

These calculations were destroyed by the Spaniards themselves. Under the pressure of the Spanish nobility and clergy, Charles II, in his will of November 1700, named the Duke of Anjou, grandson of Louis XIV, as his heir, provided that the duke would assume the crown and possessions of Spain without dismemberment or partition. If the duke refused, the Austrian Archduke Charles was to be offered the crown under the same conditions. Louis XIV had little choice. If he continued to abide by the unratified treaty with England and the United Provinces, he would have to fight Spain and the imperial power, possibly with England and the United Provinces on his side. If he gave in to the Austrian demands, he would face the reality of Habsburg encirclement. If he accepted the conditions of the will of Charles II, there would

be war with Austria, the United Provinces and England, but
Spain would be on his side. Louis also reasoned that possibly,
with the separation of the French and Spanish crowns assured, England and Holland might remain at peace.

Therefore Louis XIV believed that he stood at least a
chance of having to fight only the Austrian Habsburgs. But
the Habsburg armies, without a declaration of war, had
penetrated Italy on arrival of the news of Charles II's death.
Louis accepted what now appeared to be the inevitable and
sent French troops into the Spanish Netherlands. Despite
all previous statements to the contrary, England and the
United Provinces feared that this was but the first step in
an eventual union of the Spanish and French crowns. Louis'
announcement that this was done to protect the Netherlands
until the new Spanish monarch should be able to take
possession did nothing to allay their suspicions. The French
began mobilization in June, and Louis negotiated an alliance with Spain in September. All that remained for open
warfare to commence was the recalling of diplomatic representatives. By the spring of 1702 William III of England
had organized a grand alliance against France that consisted
of England, the Holy Roman Empire, the United Provinces,
and Savoy, for the purpose of placing the younger brother
of the Austrian Habsburg heir on the Spanish throne. The
allied nations simply did not trust Louis XIV or his heirs
to maintain the separation of France and Spain. On the
other hand, the Habsburgs had maintained the separation
of the imperial and Spanish possessions since the abdication
of the Emperor Charles V in 1556. Even if the Habsburgs
were one day to reunite Spain and the Empire, the threat
to England and the United Provinces would be far less than
any union of France and Spain. The contiguous European
land power of a united France-Spain, when added to the
Spanish colonial empire and combined Franco-Spanish naval
strength, might well have proven irresistible. It is no

wonder that Louis XIV was looked upon as a threat to all of Europe after he accepted the testament of Charles II of Spain. The government of France during the War of the Spanish Succession was that of royal absolutism. Louis XIV had carried on the work of political centralization begun by Henry IV and advanced by Richelieu and Mazarin. Under Louis XIV absolute monarchy reached its height in France. He made the government a personal monarchy—a government in which the king is the sole authority. The life of France centered on Louis XIV, who adopted the sun as his symbol and received the nickname of the Sun King. Although Louis did not have a brilliant mind, he was a hard working monarch who attempted to superintend personally the major departments of the royal government. He regarded his ministers merely as his assistants to carry out his ideas.

There was a darker side to the bright picture made by Louis XIV and his dazzling court at Versailles. This was the plight of the nation as a whole. By 1701 the warlike policies had already gravely weakened France. The country needed peace and prosperity to return to a sound financial basis and to overhaul the social system which permitted much of the nation's wealth to go untaxed. There were those in France who saw the social and economic ruin that would overtake their country unless reforms were carried out in an energetic manner. The nobles and the higher clergy, who consumed so much and contributed so little to the well being of the state, were exempt from the most burdensome taxes. Louis unfortunately had not the moral courage or inclination to make the needed reforms. When Racine, in *Esther* and *Athalie,* added open expressions of sympathy for the peasants in his rather thinly veiled references to dictators, Louis was annoyed that a mere poet should criticize his government and banished Racine from Versailles. Fénelon received much the same treatment when it was realized that *Télémaque's* purpose was to impress realization of the regime's most flagrant abuses upon the young Duke of Burgundy. A few years later, in 1707, Vauban, in his *Dîme royale,* advanced a plan to eliminate tax exemptions and thus compel the nobles and clergy to contribute their share. For years Vauban had vainly urged reform, but when he finally published the book it was burned, and Louis XIV's greatest military tactician died in disgrace. With these three examples before their eyes it was little wonder that the lesser and more cautious men of the court and country did not attempt reform during the War of the Spanish Succession. This lack of action, coupled with an inefficient and corrupt administration and the refusal of the upper classes to realize the need of reforms, caused France to commit military, economic and social suicide during the War of the Spanish Succession.

The 150,000-man army of France on entering the War of the Spanish Succession was not the superb fighting force that has often been portrayed. In 1701 it was barely midway in transition from the feudal mass of the pre-Bourbon period to the precision organization of the mideighteenth century. Actually, not until the days of Napoleon would the army of France become standardized even in numbers of men in units, in tactics, and in recruitment methods. Lack of tactical standardization within the army gave local commanders the initiative to try out and perfect new methods of fighting.[1] With each unit commander using his own style of training it is remarkable that any field commander was able to make an efficient fighting force out of a composition of different sized units that shaded in quality from excellent to ridiculous. It was quite impossible in the War of the Spanish Succession for a French general to derive more than a vague notion of the size of his army from tables of organization

[1] Villars, *Traité de la guerre de campagne,* Bibliothèque Nationale (hereinafter cited as BN), AF6257. Also see Louis Etienne Dussieux, *L'Armée en France* (Versailles, 1884), II, 187-93. The key to tactical standardization before the French Revolution lies with the infantry.

and equipment. The generals were forced to count noses after arriving in the field to command an army where a battalion might have sixty or six hundred men.

Many mistaken notions have arisen on the standardization of tactics and military administration in this period. The real story of French military development during the reign of Louis XIV lies in the immaturity of the French army by 1700. While it is true that the Marquis of Louvois did bring the army effectively under the royal thumb and provide such things as common uniforms, marching in step, and weapons, he certainly did not establish a mature system of administration.[2] The logistics and ordnance functions of the French army were not standardized until the Napoleonic period.[3] When one realizes that during the War of the Spanish Succession France was fighting concurrently in the colonies, in Flanders, on the Moselle, along the Rhine and the Rhone, and in Spain, from time to time supplying money to Charles XII of Sweden, the Hungarian rebels, and the Ottoman Empire and that there were at least thirty provincial intendants filing reports and making requests concerning everything from the azalea crop to the conduct of the local companies of militia, the vastly complicated problem of the war department logistical system begins to emerge. Then to the normal duties of the Minister of War must be added the necessity of running the war and maintaining some coordinated effort among the farflung armies. In reality all Louvois did was to collect the strands of war into one office, and by 1700 that office had become incomprehensible for any one man.[4]

Another mistake has been to assume that because of

[2] Archives Nationales (hereinafter cited as AN), M639, Cahiers 1 a, e. The most concise statement of the maturity of the French Army will be found in Richard A. Preston and others, *Men in Arms* (New York, 1956), 112ff.

[3] AN AD6, Dossiers 1, 2, 4, 16.

[4] This conclusion is based on materials contained in the Archives de la Guerre (hereinafter cited as AG), *Mémoires techniques, 1701* and *1705* and the AN AD6, Dossiers M638-40, 643, 647, 659.

Vauban's fortress-magazine system the standard tactic of the late seventeenth and early eighteenth centuries was siege warfare. This was not true. The greatest generals of the period, Prince Louis of Baden, Eugene of Savoy, the Duke of Marlborough, and Marshal Villars preferred open combat and used lightning-fast maneuvers wherever possible. A secondary theme of this present work is to demonstrate the surprising mobility of the various armies involved and to show how these armies were highly adaptable to trench, siege, and line-of-battle operations. The commonly supposed mentality of the star fortress fades into the background as, time after time, a general leaps far past his fortress-depot to live off the land and to take the war to the homeland of the enemy.

In order to defeat the powerful coalition of his enemies, Louis XIV needed the talents of the great men of the previous generation. But Vauban, Luxembourg, and Louvois were no longer on the scene. The Marquis of Chamillart, the most capable administrator of Louis XIV during the War of the Spanish Succession, had the burden of being both the Controller General of Finance and the Minister of War. He also lacked the immense personal authority of Louvois and was looked upon as the favorite of Madame de Maintenon.

It was the king himself, at the price of immense labor and by assuming tasks far too arduous for a man of sixty, who took the responsibility of planning the campaigns and ordering the generals on all fronts from his desk at Versailles. What this form of centralized control meant to the field commanders is easily calculated. Couriers must have ridden countless horses to death carrying the daily reports of Tallard, Vendôme, Villars, and others to Versailles and returning with detailed plans to the battlefields in Spain, Italy, Germany, and the Low Countries. Certainly such mediocre marshals as Villeroi, Tallard, La Feuillade, and Catinat had need of detailed orders for they were incapable of independent action. But this "cabinet system" of command was deplorable when applied to competent generals such as Vendôme and Villars.

But of all the officers named only one had the necessary courage to disobey the king and the luck that comes only from great ability to reap victory from disobedience. Perhaps only a man who had matured amid the rapid changes and confusion within the French army in the last score of years of the seventeenth century could understand the clumsy, complicated mechanism of the war machine and make it work, at least in one specific theater of operations at a time.

It is contended that Claude Louis Hector de Villars was that man. That he rose to be called duke, brother, and commanding general of the camps and armies of the king is indeed surprising; for he was born (May 8, 1653) into a party—The Frondeurs—inimical to the king and was the grandnephew of Marshal Bellefonds, hated by Louvois, the minister of war. In 1654 Pierre de Villars, Claude's father, came under the protection of the Prince of Conti. Desiring a military career, Pierre obtained a lieutenant general's commission only to find that the Marquis of Louvois refused him an assignment. Stopped short at the outset of his military career, Pierre de Villars entered the foreign service and in time became ambassador successively to Denmark and to Spain. Fortunately Pierre's personal friendships with Mesdames de Sévigné, de Scarron, and de Maintenon opened the necessary doors for young Claude, despite the towering rage of Louvois and the mistrust of Louis XIV for all the families of the Fronde.[5]

At the age of seventeen, after education at the Oratorian

5 The information contained in the next few pages on the early years of Villars is summarized from Charles Jean Melchoir, marquis de Vogüé, *Mémoires du duc de Villars* (Paris, 1884), Vol. 1; Louis Pierre Anquetil, *Vie du maréchal duc de Villars* (Paris, 1787), Vol. 1; and Guillaume la Pause, abbé de Margon, *Mémoires du duc de Villars* (La Haye, 1758), Vol. I.

College in Juilly and the Corps of Pages of the Grand-Equerry, Claude de Villars was designated to accompany his uncle, the Count of Saint-Geran on a diplomatic mission to Brandenburg. His granduncle Marshal Bellefonds recalled him as an aide-de-camp for the Dutch campaign in 1670, but Louvois refused to sign the commission. Undaunted, young Villars entered the army as a second lieutenant of cavalry and was cited for bravery at Zutphen by Monsieur, the king's brother. In this same battle Monsieur de la Rochefoucauld, first lieutenant of the Burgundian light cavalry, was killed. Villars hastily solicited his place, and Louis XIV expressed delight that the young man dared to request a favor and did not cringe in his royal presence.

This promotion gave Villars a place in the *Maison du Roi*. Joining the Army of the Rhine with his regiment, Villars was cited for skill and bravery by the great Turenne. After the campaign Louis XIV dispatched him as a courier to Madrid as a sign of his favor. In Spain Claude was reunited with his family, and the meeting has been described as at first joyous but later somber when he informed his family that he would rise through the ranks by his own ability, bravery, and audacity without regard to the safety of his person.

In 1673 young Villars served before Maestricht, whose siege Louis XIV personally directed. One day Villars ignored a superior's orders and led a cavalry charge. When called into the royal presence and reprimanded by the most august Louis XIV, Villars did not even bow but boldly proclaimed with sweeping gestures that he had disobeyed only because the king favored the infantry and that he, Villars, wished to bring the bravery of the cavalry to the royal attention. Louis was enraptured and wrote in the margin of the bravery citation signed by Turenne, *"Comme celui d'un jeune officier qu'il falloit avancer."* The very next year at Seneffe, Villars refused to leave the field of battle although wounded in three places. As a result, the Prince of Conti cited him for excellent conduct under fire. Thus at twenty-one the future marshal had six citations, three wounds, and the rank of first lieutenant. In recognition of such an unusual record Louis XIV named Villars colonel of the cavalry regiment of Courcelles. It is of passing interest that the lieutenant colonel of this regiment was the son of Madame de Sévigné. In Flanders, at Bouchain and Aire, under Condé, Claude received his fourth wound and nearly died from dysentery while in the hospital at Charleroi.

The next year before St. Omer, Villars disobeyed a direct order of De Chamlay and ordered a charge by the entire left flank of the French cavalry. Fortunately for his future career this charge broke the right flank of the army of the Prince of Orange. Had it not been for his success, Villars would have received far worse punishment than his official reprimand from Marshal Soubise. In 1675, Villars' regiment was sent to Alsace for service in the army of Marshal Créqui. When at one point the imperials under the able Prince of Baden breached the leading French columns, Créqui charged the reserve cavalry, and Villars finished the charge on foot after having two horses shot from under him. Créqui crossed the Rhine at Neuf Brisach and marched on the fortress of Kehl. Finding that he had insufficient men and materials to invest Kehl properly, Créqui decided upon a frontal assault of Freiburg. Villars was given the position of leading colonel in the cavalry forward screen. In the gorge of Waldkirch, Villars ambushed a thousand fusiliers of the Duke of Lorraine. Freiburg was taken by direct, bloody, scalingladder assault and not by constricted siege warfare. In his report Créqui cited Villars.

In 1678, with Créqui still on the Rhine, Villars was again cited. Then in 1679 Marshal Schomberg cited Villars, but the hatred of Louvois and perhaps the mistrust of Louis XIV persisted. A personal interview with the king yielded Villars nothing. In the winter of 1678-1679 Villars reportedly resolved to force a promotion for himself or die in the next campaign. Fortunately peace intervened.

Besides marking the high point of the military fortunes of Louis XIV, the Treaty of Nimwegen (1679) seemed to assure the peace of Europe for a long time. Reduced to inaction when he considered that he was beginning to be noticed, Villars saw with disgust that his ambitions would have to wait. Returning to Paris, he was graciously received in the home of Madame de Sévigné, who, in order that her son's friend might present a proper appearance, settled 1,000 pistoles per annum on the young colonel. As late as 1686 we find Villars engaged in the frivolous life that centered in the Court. But Villars, by this date, was well aware that he was thirty-three years old and still a colonel with no hope of promotion. Looking around, he found that there was only one place in all of Europe where war raged, and that was in Hungary. Many Frenchmen were volunteering their services to the Habsburg emperor to fight against the Turks. Villars decided to go.

To Villars' disappointment, Louis XIV would not at first grant him permission. But his friends at the court obtained for him the job of carrying the condolences of the French court to Austria on the death of Anne of Austria, sister of the Emperor Leopold. Villars found himself favored by the ever-expanding influence of Madame de Maintenon, who according to rumor had been a mistress of his father in earlier years. Besides his official duties in Vienna, Villars was given the job of keeping the new Elector of Bavaria, Max Emmanuel, loyal to his French alliance. In Vienna, Villars became the fast friend of the generous elector, who invited him to come to Munich for an extended period and sample the delights of his electoral court. After Villars had been in Munich for two months, the Franco-Bavarian alliance was as firm as cast iron. Louis XIV was so well satisfied that he made Villars his representative to the electoral court.

Shortly afterwards Max Emmanuel decided to lead the Bavarian army against the Turks. Villars asked for permission to accompany the elector, a request to which Louis XIV readily agreed. On June 1, 1687, the Elector of Bavaria gave Villars command of many squadrons of the Bavarian cavalry, and on August 12 Villars led the Bavarians as a unit in the grand charge which defeated the Ottoman Empire in the battle of Zenta. But unfortunately for the future reputation of Villars, who was personally cited by Prince Eugene, the elector, feeling slighted, collected his troops and went home. Villars returned to Munich with Max Emmanuel and continued in his capacity as representative of the king until the War of the League of Augsburg replaced him in his proper environment.

In 1689 Villars was promoted to the rank of brigadier general of cavalry for action around Valcourt, upon the recommendation of Marshal Humières. It was a promotion that came not only for his personal bravery but also as a result of admiration for his audacity in the face of the enmity of the powerful Louvois and the mistrust of the king for all those of the Fronde. In 1691 Villars, as general, commanded the cavalry of Marshal Luxembourg and was promoted to lieutenant general after effecting the capture of Prince Louis of Baden at Visloch. It was more than chance that this promotion came immediately after Louvois' death in 1691. In 1693 he was made inspector general for the armies of France by Louis XIV and admitted to the order of the *Cordon Bleu*. Catinat cited Villars for bravery in 1696 for his actions in the Italian campaign of that year. When Pierre de Villars died in 1697, Claude assumed the family title of marquis.

It was known throughout Europe that Ryswick had settled nothing and was only a truce to give the various powers time to consider the enormous problem of the forthcoming succession in Spain. With the conclusion of peace Lieutenant

General Villars was sent as ambassador to the imperial court in Vienna, a post he was to retain until the beginning of the War of the Spanish Succession. It may be remarked that save for brief intervals Villars had spent his entire adult life on the field of campaign and that he had risen from the grade of second lieutenant to lieutenant general, despite grave handicaps of birth and family, in a time when the sons of many noble families began their military careers as aides-de-camp with a rank of at least lieutenant colonel. He had personally experienced the terror and the joy of battle and had obtained that understanding of the common soldier that comes only after long years of close association. His motto was, "Audacity—always audacity." In the forthcoming chapters we shall see how this motto blazed forth on the battlefields of the War of the Spanish Succession.

CHAPTER TWO

A Baton Gained, 1701-1702

.

IN THE SPRING OF 1701 LOUIS XIV ISSUED HIS FIRST CAM-
paign orders for the War of the Spanish Succession. In the
Spanish Netherlands and in the Milanese he would occupy
as much territory as possible; on the Rhine the French army,
in cooperation with the forces of the Elector of Bavaria,
would wage a vigorous offensive. When apprised by Villars
from Vienna early in March that the Habsburg armies were
moving, the French king ordered his regulars to report and
dispatched the first of many calls for the militia. In May
Villars was informed that the Prince of Baden was to command on the Rhine and Prince Eugene would direct the
campaign in Italy. Villars was ordered home on July 18.
Count von Zinzendorf immediately left Versailles for Vienna.
After reporting to the king, Villars was assigned as chief-of-
staff to Marshal Catinat in Italy. The lieutenant general was
not overly happy at being second in command to a man he
considered wholly incompetent.[1]

The hearty welcome given Villars by the common soldiers
of the Army of Italy denoted their respect for him. His brave
deeds and his reputation for good fortune, wit, and jocular
humor made him very popular. When he rode into the

camp at Pizighettone, he was received with shouts of accla-
mation. At the same moment that he entered Catinat's camp
a party of enemy horsemen appeared. Villars seized the reins
of a fresh horse from a startled officer, collected whatever
cavalry he could and, without regard to formation or tactics,
rushed out to meet the imperials who, only scouts, turned
and ran from such a spirited offensive. When Villars rejoined the army in its new position at Ogilio, the enthusiasm
of the soldiers knew no bounds. But Catinat moved with a
slowness unusual even for him, and Villars had no further
chance to show his mettle. Fortunately for him, when
Villeroi replaced Catinat in late August and suffered the
defeat of Chiari (September 1), Villars was on detached duty.
The lieutenant general was glad to return to Versailles when
the Army of Italy entered winter quarters in early November.[2]

Events had moved forward rapidly on the other fronts.
Villeroi had spent most of the summer marching and counter-
marching along the Rhine, all the while pleading that he
lacked supplies of every kind. After being replaced in Italy
by Villeroi, Catinat, now commanding in Alsace, promptly
established his camp near Metz and refused even to maneuver for the rest of the campaigning season, writing requisitions for reinforcements and supplies of all kinds. Only
in the Spanish Netherlands did Louis XIV obtain any
success. There Marshal Boufflers struck before the Dutch
could reinforce their weak battalions and overran the barrier fortress.

At Versailles the king greeted Villars warmly and, to his
intense satisfaction, announced that he had reserved for him
command of the army that was to march into Germany to
aid the Elector of Bavaria. During the winter months at

1 Villars to Chamillart, May 4, 23, AG 1596; Barbesieux to Baretin, May
8, AG 1596.
2 Villars to Chamillart, November 16, 18, 19, AG 1596; De Vogüé, Mémoires,
II, 1-12.

Versailles, Villars' eyes turned, at the age of fifty, to An-
gélique Roque de Varangeville, a very beautiful and immensely rich ward of the king. He quickly married her, and
before his return to the field of battle he had sired an heir.
Although very happy, he found that the difference in their
ages, the obvious condition of his wife, and the recentness
of their vows led many court gossips to imply the worst.[3]

Fortunately, before the hot-tempered lieutenant general
could challenge any of the gossipmongers to a duel, the
campaign of 1702 opened on the Rhine. Despite Louis
XIV's promise, Villars received orders to join Catinat. There
he was given command of an army of observation and sent
to the Saar. Six months were lost between Metz and Strasbourg while the inert and indecisive Catinat allowed the
Prince of Baden's army to seize Haguenau and Wissembourg and to besiege Landau. During this period Villars
barraged the court with letters asking for an independent
command and soundly criticized Catinat for not relieving
the siege of Landau. Catinat, in his turn, complained bit-
terly to Chamillart that Villars was jeopardizing the entire
Rhine operation by his refusal to hold the Saar and his
insistence upon independent action. As a result of this
bickering Villars was summarily ordered to hold the bridges
across the Rhine in his sector and told that the king preferred Marshal Catinat's advice to that of Lieutenant General Villars. However by late August 1702, Chamillart wrote
Villars that the king admitted that Catinat had been wrong
in not pursuing a more vigorous campaign and that he,
Villars, had been right.[4]

Villars was camped at Drusenheim on September 2 when

3 Louis de Rouvroy, duc de Saint-Simon, *Mémoires*, ed. by A. M. de
Boislisle (Paris, 1879), X, 20ff; Philippe de Courcillon, duc de Dangeau,
Journal, ed. by Feuillet de Conches (Paris, 1854-1860), VIII, 299ff; De
Vogüé, *Mémoires*, II, 13.
4 Villars to Chamillart, June 14, July 8, 16, 28, August 2, 8, 22, AG 1572;
Catinat to Villars, July 30, August 7, AG 1582, 1569; Catinat to Louis XIV,
August 20, AG 1569; Chamillart to Villars, July 31, August 3, AG 1582, 1569.

he received an order from the king commanding him to
lead an army of penetration into the Empire and to link
up with the forces of Max Emmanuel, the Elector of Bavaria.
This offensive plan was well suited to the character of the
lieutenant general. But knowing well the jealous nature of
Max Emmanuel, he did not deceive himself that the campaign would present no difficulties. Villars believed, however, that during the War of the League of Augsburg the
personal bravery of the Bavarian prince had often made
amends for his deficiencies in tactics. On his side, Max
Emmanuel considered Villars a jealous and vain man but at
the same time an admirable tactician. Obviously Louis XIV
ignored this possible clash of personalities because he felt
that of all his generals only Villars could deal with his sensitive ally.[5]

From a military point of view the task set for Villars and
the Elector of Bavaria could hardly have been a more difficult one. While the imperials steadily reinforced their
garrisons along the Rhine, the defense of Landau weakened.
"Landau cannot last long," Villars wrote Chamillart while
estimating in vivid detail what he thought the forthcoming
campaign should and could accomplish. First, a passage
should be forced across the Rhine at Hüningen joining forces
with the Elector of Bavaria. The combined Franco-Bavarian
army should march rapidly along the right bank of the
Danube, assuring its line of retreat and establishing a communications link with the Army of Italy; then, by the use
of pontoon bridges and an *attaque brusquée,* force the capitulation of Ulm, Donauwörth and Ingolstadt. Next, cavalry
units should be sent on independent missions to scourge
as much of Austria as possible. At this moment the Army
of the Rhine, in Alsace, should launch a full scale offensive

5 Chamillart to Villars, August 30, AG 1569; Nicholas Catinat, *Mémoires
et correspondance,* ed. by M. Bernard (Paris, 1819), III, 185ff; Leander
Heinrich Wetzer, *Spanischer Successions-Krieg. Feldzug 1702* (Vienna, 1887),
491-502.

while the bulk of the imperial forces would be hurrying south to defend Vienna from what would appear to be an attempt to penetrate the Habsburg stem duchies.[6]

For such an audacious plan to succeed the greatest co-operation and diligence was needed between Villars, Max Emmanuel, Catinat on the Rhine, Vendôme in Italy, and the ministry in Versailles. It was also necessary for the penetration to begin while a large portion of the imperial army was tied down before Landau. By extremely good fortune the garrison in besieged Landau continued to resist. But the plan began to fall apart even before Villars could begin his march. The Elector of Bavaria started only a small force under the command of the Count of Arco to meet Villars, and on September 8 Max Emmanuel turned up before Ulm with the bulk of the Bavarian army. Ulm fell in six hours. But on September 9, after eighty-four days of con-tinuous bombardment, the garrison of Landau capitulated. The Prince of Baden was now free to maneuver. After secur-ing Landau and his fortified positions, Prince Louis recrossed the Rhine and moved south.[7]

The news that Landau had fallen and that the Prince of Baden was moving south filled the Elector of Bavaria with uneasiness. Fearing a possible attack on his own territories, Max Emmanuel ordered the Count of Arco to countermarch —without first informing Villars. To compound this tactical error, the Count of Locatelli, who carried the news to Catinat, was taken prisoner by an Austrian cavalry patrol. The im-perials now knew that Villars would not receive aid from the Bavarian army. Villars during this time, consumed with impatience, waited at Strasbourg for the reinforcements that never arrived. Messages continued to come from the elector promising to march from one day to the next. One of these

6 Villars to Chamillart, September 11, AG 1582; Villars to Chamillart, June 25, AG 1568, details the original plan.
7 Villars to Chamillart, September 11, 13, AG 1582; Catinat to Louis XIV, September 14, AG 1570; Chamillart to Villars, September 18, AG 1582.

messages was intercepted by the soldiers of the Count of Fürstenburg and passed on to the Prince of Baden who, in full knowledge of the elector's actual position, sensed a falling out among the enemy. Finally on September 22 the Marquis of Luttens, aide-de-camp to the elector, arrived in the camp of the Army of the Rhine. He verbally informed Catinat that the Count of Arco had advanced as far as Stühlingen (thirteen miles from the Rhine) and would await there for reinforcements from the French army. It was the wish of his Serene Electoral Highness that Villars rush to Arco's aid.[8]

Catinat did nothing until a dispatch bearing the signet of the king ordered him into action. Even if the elector failed to live up to his treaty obligations, Louis XIV would support his ally. He ordered Catinat to form a strong detachment of his best troops and to place them under the command of Lieutenant General Villars, who would force a passage of the Rhine at Hüningen not later than the second of October. Louis also stated that the elector had agreed to aid Villars' passage by a powerful diversionary action on the right bank of the Rhine.[9]

When Catinat's courier arrived, Villars put his plan into operation. His force of thirty battalions and forty squadrons, supported by thirty pieces of cannon, as he reported to Versailles, was composed of the best troops he had seen in thirty years of military life, who were anxious to take the field after six months of inactivity. "In truth, Sir," Villars wrote Chamillart, "the armies of the king are well trained, numerous, filled with valor, and ready to give battle to His Majesty's enemies. I wish to take the liberty of saying that nothing is impossible for these men. For such men the pri-

8 Catinat to Louis XIV, September 21, 22, AG 1570; Villars to Chamillart, September 23, AG 1582; copy of the report of Luttens to Catinat, September 22, AG 1582; Elector of Bavaria to Catinat, September 23, AG 1582.

9 Chamillart to Villars, September 23, AG 1582; Catinat to Louis XIV, September 23, AG 1570; Louis XIV to Catinat, September 25, AG 1570.

mary and only action is to meet the enemy on the field of battle." This was an expression of Villars' doctrine of war. A war of siege, however adventuresome and honorable, left little initiative for the individual commander. Villars preferred a war of movement where he might bring his second military dictum into play. He believed that not only must the field of battle be won but the enemy army's will to resist must also be broken beyond repair.[10]

While the columns of his army marched along their designated routes, Villars rode on ahead. On September 28, he arrived at Hüningen and wrote to the elector: "My Lord, it was with deep humiliation that I received the orders from His Majesty to march with all possible speed to your aid. I am very impatient in my ardor for service with a man whom I have known and respected for many years." Villars continued by telling the elector the size of his force, adding that he had forty loaded ammunition wagons, 1,000 extra horses, and 100,000 écus for the Bavarians. When his force was joined by that of the elector, Villars expected to make things very difficult for the Holy Roman Emperor.[11]

On the next day Villars surveyed the countryside. Hüningen was a watch post built by Vauban in a hexagonal pattern, elevated on piers on the left bank of the Rhine which actually washed against one wall. At this point the Rhine was separated into two branches by a large island, on which could be seen the ruins of fortifications destroyed under the terms of the Peace of Ryswick. The larger branch (about 600 feet wide and filled with rapids) was nearer the fortress. The smaller, which was less than 200 feet wide, was shallow enough for cavalry. Once past the island the Rhine flowed through a flat plain for about one and one-half miles; then,

10 Villars to Chamillart, September 26, AG 1582; Chamillart to Villars, September 28, AG 1582.
11 Relation of march orders and movements of the Bavarian army after the fall of Ulm to September 26, AG 1582; Villars to the Elector of Bavaria, September 28, BN 296.

after another sharp drop, it ran through a larger, forested plain. This second plain was bordered by a range of low hills, the highest of which was terraced with grapevines and crested by the small village of Tülingen. In this very strong position the Prince of Baden waited with a large force of imperials.[12]

Villars rapidly drew up his battle plan. On September 29 he quietly placed two companies of infantry and a party of engineers on the island. Covered from surprise attack by the infantry, the engineers set to work to repair the fortress. At the same time, under cover of the cannon of Hüningen, Villars ordered construction of a bridge of boats spanning the two branches of the river. The bridge, despite constant imperial harassment, was finished by October 2, and two companies of grenadiers entrenched themselves on the right-bank approaches.[13]

In the midst of these active preparations for battle, Villars received a message which angered him. Max Emmanuel informed him that he, the Elector of Bavaria, had decided not to join his army with the French forces on the Rhine but proposed instead to aid the army of Marshal Vendôme in holding the mountain passes of the Tyrol. Disappointed and discontented, Villars dashed off a letter to Louis XIV in which he castigated the elector. But before Louis XIV could answer, a letter arrived from Chamillart which somewhat appeased Villars' anger. Chamillart had started a reinforcement of ten battalions and twenty squadrons on their way and urged Villars to take the offensive as soon as possible.[14]

As a result of being reduced to his rather small force and

12 Villars to comte d'Arco, September 29, in Charles Jean Melchoir, Marquis de Vogüé, *Villars d'après sa correspondance* (Paris, 1888), II, 266ff· Villars to Chamillart, September 30, AG 1582; De Vogüé, *Mémoires*, II, 27ff.

13 Catinat to Chamillart, October 1, AG 1570: Puyzieulx to the Elector of Bavaria, September 30, BN 498; Villars to Chamillart, October 2, 3, 5, AG 1582.

14 Louis XIV to Villars, October 5, AG 1582; Chamillart to Villars, October 5, AG 1582; Villars to Chamillart, October 7, AG 1582; Elector of Bavaria, October 8, AG 1582; Catinat, *Mémoires*, III, 179.

deprived of the advantage of a diversion by the Elector of Bavaria, Villars was faced with a delicate and extremely dangerous operation. Any attempt to cross the Rhine on the single narrow bridge of boats with all his army and form in line of battle on the small plain would place every French soldier within easy range of the Prince of Baden's artillery with no hope of immediate retaliatory fire. Unknown to Villars, Prince Louis had an almost equal amount of infantry. But possession of the high ground and an overwhelming number of cavalry more than made up for the admitted fighting superiority of the French line. One part of the imperial infantry occupied Tülingen and the high ground. The imperial squadrons were massed at the bottom of the larger plain, and their front was defended in the middle by Fort Friedlingen and at either end by a heavily garrisoned redoubt.[15]

Choosing a moonless night, Villars sent several parties of engineers onto the small plain with the idea of digging entrenchments and clearing avenues for his cavalry. The imperial cavalry learned of their presence and tried to dislodge these work parties throughout the night, but the protecting infantry units stood their ground despite heavy losses. Recognizing the impossibility of crossing the Rhine at this point without heavy losses and possible disaster, if the bridge of boats should give way under the heavy imperial fire, Villars determined to seek a crossing elsewhere. To keep the Prince of Baden occupied, the French engineers continued working while small parties of infantry rushed over the bridge at irregular intervals. At dusk on October 11 a detachment composed of 2,000 infantry and two regiments of dragoons entrenched themselves on the heights of Nürnberg, a small place within imperial-held territory some twenty-one miles

---

15 Villars to Chamillart, October 9, AG 1582; Villars to Louis XIV, October 9, AG 1582; Louis Pelet (ed.), *Mémoires militaires relatives à la succession d'Espagne sous Louis XIV*, extraits de la cour et des généraux (Paris, 1862), II, 394-98.

down the Rhine. On the following night, after building a bridge of boats without arousing the suspicion of the imperials, this detachment silently crept up the walls of a nearby castle and carried the 400-man garrison without firing a shot. On the next day Villars gathered the rest of his troops and sailed down the Rhine to Nürnberg. There he planned to build a second bridge.[16]

On his arrival Villars found a letter waiting for him from the Elector of Bavaria. Changing his mind again, Max Emmanuel had decided to march to the Rhine after all. But finding it difficult to march as far as Hüningen, he proposed a junction of the two armies at Rothenhausen. He ended the letter by saying that he was very impatient with Villars for not coming to his aid. Containing his temper with difficulty, Villars replied in a letter calculated to appeal to the vanity of the elector. Surely, Villars wrote, a man who had not quailed at the sight of 100,000 Turks could not seriously doubt his ability to march over a few mountains. As for himself, Villars stated that he had crossed the Rhine and that all the precautions of the Prince of Baden would not deny him success. On the next day Villars wrote to Chamillart that he would attack the Prince of Baden on the morning of October 14.[17]

Certainly the diversion of Nürnberg had had its effect. Advised of the fall of the small castle and perceiving from the heights of Tülingen the movement of the French army on the Rhine, the Prince of Baden could not doubt that his adversary had found another place to cross the river. He decided to march up the river and to leave only a small holding force before Hüningen. This movement began very slowly on the evening of October 13, 1702, the cavalry soon pulling away from the footunits. The imperials were awaited

16 Villars to Chamillart, October 11, AG 1582; Villars to the Elector of Bavaria, October 13, BN 496; De Vogüé, *Mémoires*, II, 31ff.

17 Catinat to Louis XIV, October 12, AG 1570; Villars to the Elector of Bavaria, October 13, BN 496; Villars to Chamillart, October 13, AG 1582.

by a very impatient Villars. Under the cover of the long autumn night all the French infantry had crossed the Rhine, massing in the lower plain. The French cavalry was stationed on a small protrusion of the Rhine nearby.[18]

On October 14, 1702, at the first light of day, six companies of grenadiers assaulted the encampment opposite Hüningen and dislodged its few remaining defenders. At the same time the French cavalry began a long sweep along the Swiss frontier which brought them onto the large plain in battle order. Under the protection of this cavalry screen, the French battalions changed *en marche* from column to line, obviously offering pitched battle. One party of the French line marched to within gunshot of Tülingen and began chopping paths through the grapevines. The other proceeded to advance on the timbered redoubts. This maneuver was executed with speed and precision. But Villars had anticipated that the number of imperials in the fortified positions would be small as the dawn was certain to find most of the enemy units still marching for position. Such was the case. The weary imperials, after marching all night, were now faced as they swung into line of battle by the necessity of fighting a fresh French infantry already in possession of most of their own field fortifications.

Slowing down the forward movement of his cavalry, Villars put the finishing touches to his line of battle. The French right flank was aimed at Fort Friedlingen, the left rested on the hills, and the artillery was scattered up and down the line. As the French infantry came into line, they entered entrenched positions around the village. Giving

18 For various accounts of the events of October 13 and 14, 1702, centering on the battle of Friedlingen, see Villars to the Elector of Bavaria, October 14, BN 496; Puyzieulx to the Elector of Bavaria, October 12, [*sic*], BN 498; Villars to Louis XIV, October 14, AG 1582; official report of Villars to Louis XIV, October 15, BN 496; unsigned account, AG A2, II; Catinat to Chamillart and Louis XIV, October 16, AG 1570; Lieutenant General Feuguières' account, BN 9716, 223ff; Wetzer, *Feldzug 1702*, 438-77. For other informative accounts see bibliography.

command of the cavalry to Major General De Magnac, Villars placed himself in front of his line and pointed his sword toward the imperials. After a few volleys the French infantry charged and cleared the grape arbors. So closely were the fleeing imperials pressed that the fight degenerated into small-unit actions and hand-to-hand combat with heavy casualties.

During this time the plain was becoming the theater of an engagement no less violent. The imperial cavalry charged, with the Prince of Baden personally leading thirty-six squadrons of the first line. Without waiting for orders Major General De Magnac charged in his own turn. But De Magnac let the imperial cavalry line become disorganized by the length of its dash and held his own squadrons stationary until the enemy was within five hundred paces. At that instant 4,000 French heavy cavalrymen leaped upon the imperials with solid lines of flashing sabers. The effect was terrifying. After allowing their resistance to become that of a confused mob, the Germans turned and fled for the high ground. De Magnac did not follow but instead returned to his original position to await orders.

The infantry struggle now took a bad turn for the French. A bayonet fight had developed in the woods. The imperials gradually reformed as uncommitted battalions came up and stood their ground. Numerous French troops were falling— including all five brigadiers of infantry. When the woods were finally cleared, the French infantry debouched on the far side resembling more a herd of sheep than an army. Despite the urgent demands and pleadings of the few remaining officers, the numbed, confused infantrymen were slow in reforming their units. One of the lieutenants of the Prince of Baden, the Count of Fürstenberg, wisely took this opportunity to counterattack despite his relatively small force. The French infantry, taken completely by surprise and without proper leadership, broke and ran into the woods.

Within an instant the entire French line stopped, wavered, and then ran.

Fortunately Villars, from his command post, had seen the danger and then the signs of a rout. Riding quickly into the thick of battle, he cried, "Where is your courage? The battle is already won. Cry with me, 'Vive le Roi!' " But his cry was only a feeble echo against the panic of the terrified French infantrymen. Then, inspired by the god of great soldiers, Villars dismounted and seized a battle standard. Exhorting his men, he drew his pistol and turned toward the advancing imperial line. As if by magic, the French soldiers, by ones, twos, threes, and then companies and battalions, reformed in ragged lines and began to advance. The too few battalions of the Count of Fürstenberg now could do nothing but retire in good order.[19]

That same evening Fort Friedlingen capitulated to the scaling-ladder assault of the French. The imperials left 4,000 dead and wounded and twelve pieces of cannon on the field. These, when added to the official French losses of 1,152 killed and 2,389 wounded, testify to the fury of the battle. Villars ordered Brigadier General De Choisail directly to Versailles with this report: "Thirty-three standards taken without the loss of a single ensign. For the cavalry, the new regiments were as brave as the old and in the infantry the young officers covered themselves with glory." For Villars, the soldiers at evening parade cheered and cried, "Vive le maréchal! Vive le maréchal!" Louis XIV, without a murmur, ratified the battlefield promotion given by his soldiers. He sent Villars the baton of the fleur-de-lis and a personal letter of congratulation. At last the son of a Frondeur had earned the trust of the king.[20]

19 This is Villars' own account of his heroics (AG 1582, 101), but the other primary sources agree that Villars did do this, even if their judgment as to its value is somewhat different. See above, note 18.

20 Villars to Louis XIV, October 17, AG 1582; Chamillart to Villars, October 20, AG 1582; original of the marshal's commission, AG 174, 2: official French casualty list, AG 1582, 145; *Gazette de France* (October 28, 1702), 513.

To exploit this victory without delay, Louis XIV wrote to his Bavarian ally that since Villars had defeated the Prince of Baden the elector's position had changed sufficiently for him to march for a junction with the new marshal. Villars, on the afternoon of Friedlingen, wrote to Max Emmanuel that the passage of the Rhine was cleared of the enemy. On the next day Villars' cavalry patrols reported that the Prince of Baden was retiring towards Freiburg. For the next two weeks Villars wrote the Elector of Bavaria almost daily pleading with him to march for a junction while the road to the heart of the Empire lay open. He received only reports that the elector's army had not moved. It was only on October 31 that the impatient Villars received his first direct reply from the elector. Max Emmanuel was remaining on the Danube with his army but offered the petty aid of three squadrons to Villars. This communication infuriated the marshal anew, because he had lost fifteen precious days while Prince Louis was gathering troops around the walls of Freiburg.[21]

Not only did the elector fail to cooperate with his French ally; he also opened negotiations with Vienna. Finding these unsatisfactory, he presented Villars with his fourth about-face in as many months. Max Emmanuel demanded that Villars send him 10,000 of his best troops to protect Bavaria against a threatened attack by the emperor. This message did not reach Villars until November 29, by which time bad weather had set in, filling the mountain passes with ice and snow. Incapable of overcoming his mistrust for the Bavarian, he decided against further operations and wrote Louis XIV of the danger and difficulty of conducting a winter campaign in such a mountainous area and suggested that it be

21 Villars to the Elector of Bavaria, October 14, 25, 31, BN 496, October 21, 26, AG 1582. In his letter of October 31 Villars states that he has received the elector's of October 25 on this day. The general context of the elector's letter is inferred from Villars' reply. Many comments on this situation were passed between Villars, Chamillart, and Louis XIV. Most are contained in AG 1582 while a few are cited in Pelet, Mémoires, II, 420ff.

postponed until the spring. The king, much to his regret, was forced to agree and ordered Villars into winter quarters around Metz.[22]

As he had recently become a father, Villars begged for permission to spend at least two hours with his family. Louis XIV refused, and Chamillart could only relay the royal wish that Villars would remain at Metz in order to prepare the army for a spring campaign to aid the Elector of Bavaria. Finally on December 28, with all the troops installed in their winter quarters and all necessary supply requisitions for the spring already at court, Villars was allowed to return. On January 1, 1703, he arrived at Versailles overjoyed to regain the companionship of his wife and to enjoy the sight of his son.[23]

The battle of Friedlingen was the first victory for French arms in the War of the Spanish Succession. Only Villars could boast of success. Elsewhere, in the Milanese, Marshal Vendôme had no more than partial success. On the northern front, Marlborough had shown his genius by containing the far larger army of Boufflers and forcing him to retreat as far as Namur. Although it is true that Louis XIV was highly pleased with Friedlingen, it was still far too early in the war for him to realize that he had only one general with the ability to turn defeat into victory. Possibly the inability of the Bavarians and the French to cooperate had saved the

22 Villars to Louis XIV, November 1, 3, 6, 20, AG 1582; Chamillart to Louis XIV, November 3, AG 1582, maintains that the Elector of Bavaria is a very expensive ally; Villars to the Elector of Bavaria in reply to the letter of November 8, AG 1582; Villars to the Elector of Bavaria, November 12, BN 496; Chamillart to Villars, November 24, AG 1582.

23 As early as November 12 Louis XIV had decided to leave Villars in command over the winter. See Louis' margin note on AG 1582, 165; Chamillart to Villars, November 12, AG 1582; list of winter quarters for units under Villars' command, AG 1582, 199; Villars to Chamillart, November 27, AG 1582; Chamillart to Villars, December 7, AG 1582; Villars to Chamillart, December 10, AG 1582 (here another margin note gives Villars permission to return to Versailles after December 20); Elector of Bavaria to Villars, December 12, AG 1582, sends a plea for aid and a project for junction after the French army has scattered to winter quarters; Villars to the Elector of Bavaria, December 12, AG 1582.

very heart of the Holy Roman Empire from invasion and even occupation. A quick campaign sweeping along the Danube as Villars had wanted might logically have forced the Habsburgs to recall forces from other theaters of war and provided the opportunity for French successes elsewhere.

CHAPTER THREE

Disappointment and Disgrace, 1703

CONTRARY TO THE MILITARY CUSTOM OF THE TIME, LOUIS XIV reopened his campaign of 1703 in Germany in the dead of winter because the position of the Elector of Bavaria .had become critical. The Emperor Leopold had resolved to chastise the unfaithful Max Emmanuel by invading Bavaria. Menaced on three sides by imperial forces that grew stronger day by day, the elector had only 20,000 men to defend his territories. The general situation on other fronts at the beginning of 1703 was a defensive posture. In Flanders, Marlborough occupied a line along the Meuse and was with difficulty contained by Villeroi and Boufflers. Vendôme entrenched himself within the fortifications of the Milanese and prepared to ward off Prince Eugene. On the Rhine, while Tallard remained in Alsace for the purpose of defending the river, Marshal Villars was charged with forming a new army at Strasbourg to aid the embattled elector. Crossing the Black Forest in the dead of winter and traversing enemy-held territory, aided only by a hesitant ally, was the difficult task handed the new marshal.[1]

On January 15, when Villars returned to his post, most of the officers were still on leave, the regiments were down to cadre strength and the armaments were insufficient. The horses were winter lean, and the transport wagons needed weeks of work. In brief, all was disorganized—typical of an army of the early eighteenth century in winter quarters. After setting every available man to work preparing for a long, arduous winter campaign, Villars proposed that he first besiege Kehl and then assault Kinzig. Possession of these two places would put him in a valley of the Black Forest which controlled the shortest route to Bavaria. Louis XIV agreed but reminded him that the primary purpose of the winter campaign was to aid the Elector of Bavaria.[2]

Villars received a letter from Max Emmanuel on February 1 filled with recriminations which stated that he was defying the orders of Louis XIV. Villars replied that he was offended but that he would cross the Rhine on February 11 and attack the enemy wherever he could be found. If the elector would come out from behind his walls and do the same, together they might speedily put an end to the war. On February 6 it began to snow continuously. Despite this dreary, frigid weather, Villars kept his troops on the route of march. While a small diversionary detachment moved towards Haguenau the major portion of Villars' army reached Hüningen, crossed the Rhine on February 12, descended the river on the right bank, and appeared before Kehl on February 19.[3]

After dusk on February 10, 1703, Villars received word that

[1] Chamillart to Louis XIV, December 23, BN 3155; Chamillart to Villars, December 26, January 3, AG 1582, 1675; one list of the troops under Von Schlick, destined to march against the Elector of Bavaria, included 27,000 men, n.d., AG 1582, 221ff; Count of Sauvene to Chamillart, January 2, AG 1675; Villars to Chamillart, January 6, AG 1675, 1616; Ricons to Chamillart, January 10, AG 1675; extract of a letter on the imperial war plans, January 14, AG 1675.

[2] Villars to Chamillart, January 18, 19, 23, 26, 27, 29, 31, AG 1617, 1675; Chamillart to Villars, January 30, AG 1675.

[3] Elector of Bavaria to Villars, January 9, AG 1675; Villars to Chamillart, January 30, February 2, 3, 5, 7, 10, 12, 14, AG 1675; Villars to the Elector of Bavaria, January 30, February 5, AG 1675; Chamillart to Villars, February 12, 14, AG 1675; Villars to Louis XIV, February 19, AG 1675; Villars to the Elector of Bavaria, February 4, BN 496.

the Elector of Bavaria had taken the offensive and was marching up the valley of the Danube for the marshal's camp. The marshal wrote, "By my faith! I am beside myself with joy. And Your Highness shall find me the same man I was in Hungary and in Munich; beautiful women and good plays. Hurry and join me!" Villars planned to meet the Elector of Bavaria at Villingen on the Upper Danube with fifty battalions and eighty squadrons.[4]

Now Villars concentrated on Kehl. The imperials had powerfully reinforced Vauban's original fortifications with a secondary line of works. But despite the efforts of the large, high-spirited garrison the French rapidly assaulted or masked the exterior works and opened a set of parallel trenches. The fortress fell in twenty-two days after its garrison of 3,000 had been reduced by 75 percent. Kehl fell so quickly that the Prince of Baden could not even collect and start a relieving force towards the city. Present throughout the siege, urging on the soldiers by exposing himself repeatedly to the enemy fire, Villars received a high compliment for the rapidity of his attack and his method of siegecraft. Chamillart wrote that, in his opinion, Villars had learned well when he had served under Vauban. The minister went on to say that the great master of siegecraft would undoubtedly have approached the fortress in the same manner.[5]

Unfortunately the means available to Villars did not give him the opportunity to exploit his success by a rapid march into the Empire. Armaments, manpower, harnessings, and wagons were as yet insufficient for a pitched field battle. Snow continued to fall in great depth and made supply difficult by wagon and impossible by water. Suffering was

4 Villars to the Elector of Bavaria, February 10, BN 496; list of units as they came to Villars' collecting point, February 19, AG 1675.

5 Elector of Bavaria to Villars, February 20, 23, AG 1675; Villars to Chamillart, February 21-23, 26, 27, March 2-7, 9, AG 1675; Chamillart to Villars, February 26, March 1, 6, AG 1675; Villars to the Elector of Bavaria, February 26, AG 1675; Villars to Louis XIV, March 2, 10, AG 1675; Louis XIV to Villars, February 24, March 6, AG 1639.

acute among the troops because of the shortage of everything, including food and warm clothing. At the same time the French army of Marshal Tallard concentrated in Alsace did nothing, while the Prince of Baden gradually withdrew the imperial garrisons from their front to reinforce himself at Rastadt. With Prince Louis' forces greatly outnumbering his own and well supplied with every article of war, Villars for once took the path of caution and decided to retreat to a position where he could link up with the fresh troops of Tallard and at least present a unified front to the imperials. For these reasons Villars decided to countermarch his forces to Strasbourg where he might reequip them and offer his soldiers a chance to rest amid the comforts of a large city. He arrived in Strasbourg on March 18 and immediately wrote Max Emmanuel that he would arrive in Villingen on May 7.[6]

But when informing the king of his change in plans, Villars made the mistake of asking the title and honors of a duke as recompense for victory at Kehl. Louis XIV sent a letter of reprimand to his newest marshal stating that, regardless of the condition of the army, Villars would proceed either to join the Elector of Bavaria or to offer and, if necessary, force a pitched battle with the Prince of Baden. One action or the other Villars would move to accomplish without a single day's delay. Villars faced the royal anger with an icy calm. He replied in a letter filled with sarcasm, but not without a tinge of humor, that he had heard and would obey. However, he remarked, the king should be informed that the armory at Strasbourg was empty except for pikes and halberds. He was having these weapons issued to the French infantrymen as replacements. The men were "transported"

[6] Chamillart to Villars, March 9, 16, AG 1675; Louis XIV to Villars, March 6, 9, 16, AG 1675, 1639; Villars to Louis XIV, March 12, AG 1675; Villars to the Elector of Bavaria, March 12, AG 1675; Villars to Chamillart, March 14, 16, AG 1675.

with joy at the "wonderful" firepower of their new arms. While only a marshal of France, he felt that it was dangerous to offer battle with such weapons but that he would meet the Prince of Baden on the field of honor.[7]

While he argued with the king, Villars was utilizing his time to complete the outfitting of his army. Perhaps his very disagreeable and extremely dangerous exchange with the king was only a ruse by which the marshal sought to buy a few weeks to prepare his forces. The Marquis of Frézelière (lieutenant general of artillery) informed Chamillart on April 14 that Villars' actions in providing supplies for the Army of the Rhine had so thoroughly stripped Alsace that her garrisons were disarmed and useless. When Villars did move on April 16, he had gained the precious hours needed to reequip his army at the expense of his personal popularity with the king.[8]

After centering his quartermaster general at Kehl, Villars took the field with fifty-four battalions, eighty-four squadrons, forty pieces of cannon, and a supply convoy drawn by 1,200 horses. Tactically this movement did not come any too soon for the Elector of Bavaria. The circle of enemies that menaced the Bavarian frontiers was exceedingly dangerous. To the east General Schlick had taken Inn, while to the west the Count of Styrum approached the Iller River. Max Emmanuel, striking swiftly, had forced Styrum back beyond Passau and defeated Schlick. The elector was able to enter

[7] Villars to Chamillart, March 10, AG 1675; Villars to Louis XIV, March 10, 23, AG 1675; Louis XIV to Villars, March 19, AG 1675; Chamillart to Villars, March 19, AG 1675; Chamillart to Louis XIV, March 20, AG 1675; La Houssaye to Chamillart, March 23, AG 1675; De Vogüé, *Mémoires*, II, 65.

[8] This contention is based upon a lengthy series of letters in which Villars' demands for guns, bread, powder, money, and other supplies are far more persistent in the face of a royal command than was reasonable or judicious for a marshal of France during the reign of Louis XIV. That Louis did not immediately replace Villars can be explained only on the basis of need. See March 22-April 5, AG 1675 and April 6-April 13, AG 1676. On April 13 Villars announced, as if the argument had never existed, that the army was in excellent condition and spoiling for battle.

Ratisbon practically unopposed before the startled imperials had time to reform. But Max Emmanuel was fully aware that the imperials would simply call up reinforcements, while he had no reserves. As his military position deteriorated the elector wrote blunt reproaches to Villars for not hastening to his aid. Villars had simply announced that he had no intention of moving before April 1 and that he would resign his commission and retire to his estates before he would witness the loss of the war by leading a French army to certain destruction.[9]

Villars carefully proceeded up the valley of the Kinzig. Persuaded by faulty military intelligence that the marshal had only a small detachment, the Prince of Baden had only a few hussar squadrons to defend the passes. The valley itself was wide and large until the ever-climbing road became a progressively steeper path leading to Gutach, where the heavily fortified Castle of Hansach guarded the way. Reaching the town of Gutach would usually just begin the difficulties for an attacking army. Every foot of the trail from Gutach was within musket range of the castle. But the French carried Hansach at bayonet point on April 28. Then the small garrison fled without even taking time to spike the cannon or damage the powder stores.[10]

Within a few days (May 2) Villars stood before the fortress of Hornberg. The star-shaped walls of the lower works completely barred the valley. Above a second complicated series of fortifications, an old castle commanded the mountainous countryside. A forewarned garrison of 800 men stood ready to dispute the French advance. The advance guard halted before this impressive obstacle. Villars, after quickly sur-

9 Villars to Louis XIV, April 15, AG 1676; Villars' order of battle for April 13, AG 1676; Villars to Chamillart, April 16, AG 1676; Elector of Bavaria to Villars, April 11, AG 1676; Count of Lennion to Villars, April 14, AG 1676; De Vogüé, Mémoires, II, 66-77.

10 Louis XIV to Villars, April 18, 25, 27, 29, AG 1676; Villars to Louis XIV, April 21, 23, 25, 27-29, AG 1676; Villars to Chamillart, April 18, AG 1676; Chamillart to Villars, April 25, AG 1676.

veying the situation, ordered the two leading companies of
grenadiers to take the fortress. But as the incline leading
to the walls was very steep, the captains simply stared.
Villars, on seeing their hesitation leaped from his horse and
began climbing the slope, baton in hand. With a cheer, the
soldiers stormed up the slope after their marshal and carried
the outer works. The disheartened enemy garrison decamped
during the night, and Villars was the master of a serious obstacle almost without loss.[11]

The terrain continued to rise, and the French found the
climbing complicated by spring rains which turned what was
little more than a double-file footpath into a small river. The
men were obliged to march in water up to their hips and to
pull the heavy equipment through deep mud. At one point
Villars noted that it had taken fifty rounds of a twelve-
pounder to blast a rocky obstacle from the path of the army.
As the passage became more treacherous and as the discom-
forts increased, the soldiers fell mute and the usual camar-
aderie ceased. More than once the marshal dismounted to
give his horse to a common soldier who had fallen from
fatigue. Such actions could not have been without effect
on the rank and file. Villars always set an example by sharing
the dangers and hardships of every campaign.[12]

Finally, on May 4, the horizon enlarged as the plains of
the Upper Danube came into view. Two additional days
found the French before the tiny village of Villingen where
the aged Baron Wildsdorf commanded for the emperor.
When ordered to surrender, the baron refused. Villars fired
some fifty rounds into the small town and then marched
on, partially to conserve his ammunition and partially to
respect the old commandant's courage. On May 9, near

11 Villars to Chamillart, April 29, May 1, 2, AG 1676; Villars to Louis XIV,
May 2, AG 1676; Villars to the Elector of Bavaria, May 6, BN 496.
12 Villars to Chamillart, May 8, AG 1676; marquis d'Usson to Chamillart,
May 2, AG 1676; Count of Bourg to Chamillart, May 2, AG 1676; Villars to
Louis XIV, May 7, AG 1676.

Rudlingen, advanced French units contacted the escort of the Elector of Bavaria.[13]

The union of the elector and the marshal was an emotional one and quite in keeping with their respective characters. Max Emmanuel and Villars galloped towards each other, dismounted, embraced, and asked numerous questions concerning home, family, and estates. The elector did the marshal the distinct honor of having him review the Bavarian troops. The Bavarians made a very good impression on a man who knew seasoned troops that were full of fight when he saw them. That evening, after a magnificent feast, Villars unfolded a very ambitious plan before the somewhat startled Max Emmanuel. A corps composed of Bavarian infantry and a French brigade commanded by the elector would descend the right bank of the Danube to storm Passau and besiege Linz. At the head of a second corps, Villars would cross to the left bank of the Danube and defeat the Count of Styrum. The Franco-Bavarian cavalry would fan out in all directions to wreak fire and destruction wherever possible. When the two corps were reunited they would march on Vienna, moving the heavy equipment by water.[14]

During this time Marshal Vendôme, while leaving a screen on the Mincio River, marched up the Adige River and penetrated the Tyrol, where he assisted the defending Bavarian garrisons and formulated his own plan for a march on Vienna. Tallard continued to retire and by this movement drew the Prince of Baden so far into Alsace that he could not hope to succor Vienna in time, once the plans of the Franco-Bavarian army became apparent. The difficulties of the Em-

13 Elector of Bavaria to Villars, May 5, AG 1676; Villars to Louis XIV, May 7, AG 1676; Villars to the Elector of Bavaria, May 7, BN 496; Villars to Chamillart, May 8, AG 1676; Cardinal of Fürstenberg to Chamillart, May 12, AG 1676. The relative ease and the unusual secrecy with which Villars accomplished this remarkable march can be readily seen in the *Mercure historique et politique*, XXXIV (May 1703), 513-16, 528-31, whose informants placed Villars somewhere in Baden.

14 Villars to Louis XIV, May 16, AG 1676; project of Villars, May 16, AG 1676; Dangeau, *Journal*, IX, 196ff; De Vogüé, *Mémoires*, II, 85ff.

peror Leopold, caused by the Hungarian revolt, occupied a great number of imperial troops and left Vienna with an undermanned garrison. Only the army of Styrum and fortified towns stood between Villars and Vienna. But the success of the operation depended upon many loosely connected factors: the continued cooperation of Max Emmanuel and Villars, Chamillart's ability to hold Vendôme in check, and Tallard's continued withdrawal. At least the first of these essential conditions seemed to have been met. Max Emmanuel and his chief-of-staff, the Count of Arco, seemed pleased with the plan.

Villars regrouped both armies into the needed corps and marched it to a position in which his right was behind Dillingen, a small fortified place on the Danube, his left near Lavingen, and his front covered by a thicket. Max Emmanuel in turn led his corps back to Munich on May 16. But just as the marshal was about to begin his part of the grand strategy, a message arrived from Versailles that should have warned him of future trouble. Louis XIV had decided for political reasons that Villars must place himself under the orders of the Elector of Bavaria. At almost the same time (May 27) a letter arrived from Max Emmanuel stating that the defeat of a small Bavarian force near Amberg had uncovered Rothenburg. Because of this breach in his western line of defense, the elector renounced the plan of marching on Vienna and announced that he would stand on the defensive. Villars replied that he did not understand how the loss of three to four hundred men and three pieces of cannon could make Max Emmanuel give up a perfectly sound operational plan that would deliver the capital of the Empire to them. Surely the elector did not want to waste fifty battalions and eighty squadrons of the French army to retake one small castle when the same units might make the emperor tremble. But this was exactly what Max Emmanuel did want, and, although he was faced with the ruin of an excellent plan, Villars could do nothing but hold his position.[15]

Villars' plan was too ambitious for the early eighteenth century. Even if the Elector of Bavaria had fully cooperated, the final result would have found the Franco-Bavarian army deep within Austrian territory. There Villars would undoubtedly have had an experience similar to that which the Elector of Bavaria would soon suffer in the Tyrol. There is every reason to believe that, even if Vienna had fallen, the Emperor Leopold would have retired to Prague or some other imperial city and continued his resistance while the Habsburg forces on the Rhine and in Italy marched to encircle Villars. Such a penetration of the Austrian heartland would have required military organization and a logistical system that simply did not exist before the Napoleonic period. It is doubtful that France in 1703 possessed sufficient strength to accomplish Villars' designs without stripping the other theaters of war of men and supplies. Any such attempt would have opened the Spanish Netherlands to Marlborough and southeastern France to Eugene.

At Versailles a violent campaign was being directed against Villars by those who thought that he should obey the slightest wish of the king without hesitation. His well-known jealousy of his wife made him the brunt of many jokes. Villars now made a serious political blunder—especially for a man who had so recently tried the king's patience—by ordering his wife to join him. This was tantamount to a slap in the face for all those courtiers who inhabited the palace of Versailles. Perhaps Villars, who had participated in some of the many amours of the parasitical creatures of the court, only wanted to protect his own wife. Perhaps this was his way of snubbing the king for ordering him to take orders from

15 Villars to Chamillart, May 19, AG 1676; Villars to the Elector of Bavaria, May 20, BN 496; Elector of Bavaria to Villars, May 27, AG 1676; Chamillart to Villars, June 4, AG 1676; Gazette de France (June 2, 9, 16, 1703), 261ff, 275, 286.

Max Emmanuel and to accomplish the impossible. Whatever Villars' innermost reason may have been, he was playing a very dangerous game. Such unscrupulous characters as the Duke of Saint-Simon had written that the old marshal was so wrapped up in his young wife that he had no energy left for the battlefield. Certainly the ill-humor of such people knew no bounds. Villars wrote to his lifelong friend, the Prince of Conti, that he knew "that the terraces of Versailles have crucified me for my extravagance, my love, my avarice, and my vanity. But I say to you that I will have my way in my own family, come what may!"[16]

In eighteen months of marriage Villars had spent less than six in the company of his very amiable wife. Villars wrote Chamillart that he had no doubt that it looked, especially to all the military "experts" who never left Versailles, as if a young and beautiful woman had addled the brains of a middle-aged man. But he could not understand how the king could listen to such foolishness in the light of his past services. If it became necessary, he intended to send Madame to his estates in Dauphiné, but he would not return her to Paris. He concluded by trusting that the wisdom of the king would not force him to make a choice between "leaving his majesty's service and enjoying the company of his wife."[17]

Louis XIV, obviously not liking either this action or the haughty statement of his marshal, wrote that the extreme attachment Villars was demonstrating for his wife was detracting from the good opinion heretofore held of him. How could Villars be sure that his wife would be safe? How many squadrons would he detach to protect her? The lusts of the Elector of Bavaria were a European scandal. Such facts as this plus the standing order of "no women at the

[16] Chamillart to Villars, March 27, AG 1675; Louis XIV to Villars, March 27, AG 1639; Le Pelletier to Villars, in De Vogüé, *Mémoires*, II, 285ff; Villars to Louis XIV, March 31, AG 1675; Chamillart to Villars, April 3, AG 1675; Villars to prince de Conti, in De Vogüé, *Mémoires*, II, 288ff; Dangeau, *Journal*, IX, 191; Saint-Simon, *Mémoires*, XI, 65, 71ff.
[17] Villars to Chamillart, May 31, AG 1676.

front" had led the king to express his wish that Madame return to Paris. Furthermore, Louis promised to make a place in his own apartments for Madame Villars where she could be suitably watched.[18]

With his vehemence spent and perhaps realizing that he could ill afford to relinquish the talent of this marshal, Louis XIV wrote that Villars still possessed his complete confidence. But the king would not permit Madame to go to her husband. However, the Duke of Dangeau reports that Villars still proved so stubborn that the king finally yielded and that only the refusal of a passport by the Count of Styrum stopped Madame Villars from joining her husband. There can be no doubt that this obvious display of a rather childish desire did little to enhance Villars in the eyes of Louis XIV. True, for the present, Villars still enjoyed the king's favor, but perhaps that would not always be the case.[19]

On June 14 the changeable Max Emmanuel suddenly left Munich, stormed the fortress of Kufstein, key to the Tyrol, and by a series of rapid marches appeared before Innsbruck on June 26. This was such a brilliant success that Villars complimented the elector. But in his letter to Louis XIV the marshal claimed that Max Emmanuel's victory would cost the French Vienna. Apparently determined to follow his revised plan, the elector called for the cooperation of Vendôme. Unfortunately Vendôme was comfortably installed on the banks of Lake Garda and did not really want to campaign. With extremely bad grace he waited six weeks before even replying to the Bavarian. Prince Eugene of Savoy (recently returned to Vienna from Hungary) was not slow to profit from this respite. He reinforced the Upper Adige and armed the peasants of the Tyrol, who had been loyal to the House of Habsburg for centuries. By July 19, harassed on all

---

18 Louis XIV to Villars, June 8, AG 1676; Chamillart to Villars, June 8, AG 1676.
19 Dangeau, *Journal,* IX, 214, 216.

sides by imperial cavalry and having his small parties cut to pieces by the enraged peasantry, Max Emmanuel began to retreat. Regaining Kufstein, the Bavarian waited in vain for help from Vendôme throughout July and August.[20]

Villars was condemned to immobility for this same period on the Danube, where he held all the approaches between Ulm and Donauwörth. Consumed with irritation, impatiently awaiting the moment when he could march, and reduced to the activity of sending parties of cavalry deep into the Empire, he addressed letter upon letter to Louis XIV and Chamillart, complaining that his army was based upon air and completely isolated deep within enemy territory with faulty communications. Villars demanded that Tallard be ordered to join him with at least part of the Army of Alsace. All that he could do since no one would give him any orders or release him from Bavarian control, was to remain on the defensive and hope that the imperials would attack him. That was exactly what the Count of Styrum had in mind.[21]

On July 31 Villars' ever-active cavalry reported that an imperial detachment had crossed the Danube upstream from Ulm and was threatening his left flank. The marshal led eighteen squadrons and 700 fusiliers aboard wagons to the attack. The enemy cavalry force left eleven standards among their dead and wounded. After this rude shock the imperials became more cautious. Villars soon had his hands full repulsing the small parties who tried to burn his bridges over the Danube. By the end of August the French ammunition supply had become critical. Moreover the marshal now faced

20 Villars to Louis XIV, June 17, 30, AG 1676; Elector of Bavaria to Villars, n.d., AG 1676, 119, contains the outlines of the Tyrol campaign; Villars to the Elector of Bavaria, June 19, BN 496. For the remainder of the elector's Tyrol campaign see BN 496; letter of Eugene's intercepted by Villars, July 11, AG 1676.
21 Letters of Villars, Louis XIV, Chamillart, June 17-July 30, AG 1676. For excellent discussions of Villars' position and problems see *Gazette de France* (June 30, August 4, 1703), 309, 379; Dangeau, *Journal*, IX, 217ff, 224ff, 228ff, 237ff.

the prospect of fighting the imperial armies converging on him. The Prince of Baden was preparing a frontal assault while the Count of Styrum approached from the rear. Learning of the imperialists' plans, Villars entrenched forty-four squadrons and twenty battalions for defense of the Danube bridges and dispatched a courier to the Elector of Bavaria asking for immediate aid.[22]

Max Emmanuel rejoined Villars on September 1. A council of war ended, after a week of bitter argument, when the elector gave Villars a direct order that the combined Franco-Bavarian army march upon Augsburg. But the Prince of Baden had profited from the week's respite by marching eighty miles in three days to pass his entire army within the entrenchments of Augsburg by noon on September 5. On the evening of September 9 the marshal and the elector reconnoitered Augsburg. Judging it impossible to attack such well-manned fortifications, the Franco-Bavarian army retired. In their humiliation and anger Villars and Max Emmanuel violently castigated one another for their failure.[23]

Villars' uneasiness was doubled by the difficulty of his line of communications. As the passages of the Black Forest were in the hands of the imperials, his couriers were constantly forced to violate Swiss neutrality. It was taking five to six weeks for orders from Versailles to reach him. His material situation deteriorated each day from the lack of replacements, supplies, and money. In desperation he asked to be relieved. To add to his worries discipline problems began to emerge in the unpaid army. Villars had always imposed on his troops a very harsh discipline that many considered excessive; and, as this did not lighten the burden on the already overworked officers, several malcontents dared to complain to their friends

22 Letters of Villars, Chamillart, Louis XIV, August 6-30, AG 1676; Villars, to comte de Marsin, in De Vogüé, *Mémoires*, II, 305ff; Villars to the Elector of Bavaria, August 27, BN 496.

23 Villars to the Elector of Bavaria, September 2, BN 496; Villars to Louis XIV, September 8, 10, AG 1677; marquis d'Usson to Chamillart, September 14, AG 1677; marquis de Blainville to Villars, September 14, AG 1677.

at court and even wrote Chamillart and Louis XIV. Naturally the minister asked Villars for an explanation. Villars answered that the exacting discipline he maintained, especially the execution of looters and deserters, was all that was holding his army together. He stated that the peasants for two leagues around brought supplies to sell in his camp. This saved him much time and trouble. The king's attention was directed to the very low rate of desertion. Villars invited the minister to visit his camp.[24]

The intense irritation of all these things combined threw Villars into a state of depression. But after learning on September 17 that Styrum's army, until now immobile on the Danube, had begun to march towards Donauwörth, he decided to attack Styrum in concert with the Elector of Bavaria. He dispatched a courier to Max Emmanuel asking him to come up with all available forces. Lieutenant General D'Usson was sent with 8,000 infantry and 4,000 cavalry to cross the river and follow Styrum's route of march. On September 20, upon hearing three cannon shots at one-minute intervals, D'Usson was to attack Styrum in the rear while the combined Franco-Bavarian army assaulted from the front. The Elector of Bavaria immediately marched to Villars' aid with thirty-three battalions and forty-five squadrons. On the night of September 19 the French and Bavarians joined forces without arousing the suspicions of the imperials.[25]

Styrum was camped on a line perpendicular to the Danube

24 Louis XIV to Villars, May 24, AG 1676; Villars to Louis XIV, May 24, 30, June 4, AG 1676; Villars to the XIII Swiss Cantons, May 23, AG 1676; Count of Bourg to Chamillart, June 28, AG 1676, reports the death penalty of several hussars for desertion; Villars to Chamillart, July 1, August 25, July 12, AG 1676; marquis d'Usson to Chamillart, July 14, September 11, AG 1676; Chamillart to Villars, July 19, 30, AG 1676; Beaudouin to Chamillart, July 10, August 20, AG 1676; Chamillart to Beaudouin, July 31, 7, AG 1676.

25 For various accounts of the events centering around the first battle of Höchstädt (1703) see the official French printed account, AG A2, 11; Villars to Louis XIV, September 21, 24, AG 1677; marquis d'Usson to Chamillart, September 21, AG 1677; Pelet, *Mémoires militaires*, III, 664-75; Alphons Danzler, *Spanischer Successions-Krieg, Feldzug 1703*, (Vienna, 1878), 539-60.

with his right resting on the river and his left merging with a line of low hills. To the front stretched the plain of Höchstädt, which was flat and without any obstacles except a creek and the small village of Unterglauheim. On learning of the approaching Franco-Bavarian army, Styrum sent out advanced units and ordered them to signal the discovery of the enemy by three cannon shots spaced one minute apart. During the night, without calling attention to his presence, D'Usson had entered Unterglauheim and now waited silently behind its walls.

At 6 A.M. on September 20, 1793, three cannon shots rang out at exact one-minute intervals. D'Usson threw open the gates of the town and advanced at the head of his troops. Unfortunately it was not the French artillery that had fired the cannon. The advanced elements of Styrum's army had sighted the main Franco-Bavarian force still over two hours away. The Count of Styrum advanced his entire army against the small French force to his rear. Hurriedly reforming his line of battle into battalion-size hollow squares, D'Usson cut his way out of the rapid imperial advance. But at least six French squadrons were annihilated, and all battalions were reduced by at least 50 percent. Doggedly D'Usson fought his way back into Unterglauheim and held the town at point-blank range.

Fortunately for the besieged French, their spirited resistance had given the Franco-Bavarian army time to appear on the field of battle. Styrum was forced to break off his initial engagement in order to reform his thoroughly disorganized troops to the east. Villars, although aware of the defeat of his subordinate, was encouraged when he saw the mauled condition of many of the imperial battalions. Noting the milling and reforming going on in the enemy line, he ordered an immediate all-out attack with the cavalry charging and the infantry advancing by rolling barrage at the double time. At one wave of the fleur-de-lis baton, fifty French squadrons on the right and forty Bavarian squadrons on the left galloped toward the disorganized imperial cavalry, which took flight.

It was a different story with the imperial infantry. Encouraged by the presence of Styrum, who rode up and down fully exposing himself to the withering French fire, the imperial line retired step by step in perfect parade-ground order. At times the opposing armies were volleying at distances of less than fifty paces—a truly murderous fray for eighteenth-century armies. In fact, from 9 A.M. to 4 P.M. the German infantry withstood the continuous Franco-Bavarian mounted and foot attack without even bending, let alone breaking. Villars, tiring of this slow, retrograde movement, threw fifty-seven battalions into a sudden drum-roll attack. The exhausted imperial line doubled, and finally snapped, under the tremendous pressure of the French bayonet assault. Many of the fleeing imperials threw away their arms.

As may be imagined, casualties were high on both sides. Styrum left on the field of battle 2,000 dead and wounded and lost 3,700 prisoners, eighteen standards, fourteen flags, thirty-three cannon, and his bridge-building equipment. Accurate figures for the French losses do not exist.

Villars' report that D'Usson's force was nearly wiped out is true. But his report that the main Franco-Bavarian army lost only 500 killed and wounded must be erroneous. Possibly the known aversion of Louis XIV for bloody, pitched, expensive battles cut the French casualty list considerably. A second consideration might have been that Villars exaggerated to cast himself in the best possible light in order to regain some of his lost popularity with the king. The closest estimate that can be given after an exhaustive study of the material available would be to place the total Franco-Bavarian loss at something around 12,000 killed and wounded.[26]

This heavy French loss was due to the failure of Villars' battle plan which nearly caused the annihilation of D'Usson's

26 Villars to Louis XIV, September 24, AG 1677; *Mercure historique et politique*, XXXV (October 1703), 381-86; De Vogüé, *Mémoires*, II, 122ff.

force. It also illustrates Villars' desire for victory at any cost. A far more reasonable plan would have been to await the arrival of the artillery before attacking. Villars' unwillingness to change a battle plan once made was to cost the French many unnecessary casualties before the conclusion of the War of the Spanish Succession. The Franco-Bavarian guns were within one hour of marching time from the field. D'Usson could have held out for that long.

Villars proposed to exploit the victory without delay. He suggested to Max Emmanuel that they pursue the remnants of Styrum's army into Franconia. But the elector feared the loss of his capital city should the Prince of Baden attack from the entrenchments at Augsburg. Judging Villars' plan too dangerous, Max Emmanuel ordered the army to march on Augsburg. But when they offered battle, the Prince of Baden wisely refused to leave his fortifications.[27]

This failure at Augsburg was too much for Villars. What started out as a normal conference ended with the elector and the marshal insulting each other. This disagreement led to a final rupture between Villars and Max Emmanuel. They began to complain to Versailles of each other's conduct. Louis XIV relieved Villars of his command. The continuance of the Bavarian alliance was a political necessity. Villars was to be replaced by Marshal Marsin, who would obey the king's orders. But Louis XIV did write Villars that, despite his disgrace, he still had the greatest respect for his military ability and would find another theater where his talents would not be wasted.[28]

[27] Villars to Chamillart, September 23, 30, AG 1677; Villars to Louis XIV, September 24, 30, AG 1677; Louis XIV to Villars, September, n.d., AG 1677, again emphasized how essential the Bavarian alliance was.

[28] Villars to Louis XIV, October 3, 12, AG 1677; Louis XIV to Villars, October 8, 14, AG 1677; marquis d'Usson to Chamillart, October 11, AG 1677; Louis XIV to Marsin, October 13, AG 1677; De Vogüé, *Correspondance*, I, 268ff; Villars to Maintenon, in Saint-Simon, *Mémoires*, XI, 279ff: De Vogüé, *Mémoires*, II, 125-42, attempts to absolve his ancestor from all blame by either overlooking or ignoring things like the demand for a dukedom, the refusal to obey orders, or the wife problem.

On his return to Versailles, Villars was not welcome in the apartments of the king but found himself relegated to the life of a courtier, an existence he detested. Even more disquieting for him was the news that Marsin and Max Emmanuel had taken Augsburg and that, for the first time since the Thirty Years' War, the King of France held an important city in the heart of the Holy Roman Empire. The victory celebration which followed must have been a very bitter experience for Villars. This success was magnified by Marlborough's indecisive campaign in the Spanish Netherlands. The very fact that Marsin and Max Emmanuel could cooperate cast doubts upon Villars' military ability. Max Emmanuel's plan to defend his own territories and his successes at Ulm and Augsburg were reasonable accomplishments in the light of existing conditions. Villars' plan for 1703 was too ambitious and could not have been carried out with anything less than the concentration of all the forces of France in one theater of operations. Any such concentration, however, was impossible. His tendency to attempt the seemingly impossible, even at the risk of destroying an entire field army, certainly could not have favorably impressed Louis XIV.[29]

It seemed as though Villars' military career, so brilliant at Friedlingen and Höchstädt, had been terminated by the political manipulations of the court, the wavering personality of Max Emmanuel and his own reckless handling of his troops. The campaigns of 1702 and 1703 had demonstrated several facets of Villars' character. He had proven himself to be the most competent French general. But his insistence on having his own way regardless of the wishes of his sovereign, current high politics, and constant complaints by his subordinates made it more than necessary that Louis administer discipline to him. Pleading, orders, and threats

29 Saint-Simon, *Mémoires*, XI, 312ff, 287ff; Pelet, *Mémoires militaires*, III, 709-13.

had left Villars unmoved even after the army had moved into Bavaria. The episodes of the winter months and his unreasonable attention to his wife had angered the king. Villars obviously would not submit to the "cabinet system." The only choice left to the king was to recall him in disgrace or to give him complete liberty of action. It was obvious by the end of 1703 that Villars' dominant trait—conceit—would force the king to relegate him to the minor theaters of war as long as possible. Even now, Villars refused to beg the pardon of the king for his disobedience but instead retired to his estates in Dauphiné.

CHAPTER FOUR

The White Shirt of Revolt, 1704

IN THE SUMMER OF 1702 THE GOVERNMENT OF LOUIS XIV
had been faced with two major problems. Firstly, the long
smoldering question of the Spanish succession had blazed
into a war which found France allied with Bavaria and
Spain, opposing England, Holland and the Holy Roman
Empire. The theaters of war which had soon opened in
Flanders, Spain, Italy, and on the Rhine frontier, claimed the
primary attention and military resources of the Bourbon
monarchy. Secondly, only twelve days after France had entered the War of the Spanish Succession, a Protestant revolt
erupted in the Cévennes region of the southern French
province of Languedoc. This insurrection, known as the
Camisard Revolt, was a protest against the severe religious persecution which the government of Louis XIV had
inflicted upon Protestants with increasing regularity since
the revocation of the Edict of Nantes.[1]

For a period of over two years a body of less than 2,000
poorly armed peasants had successfully defied the power of
the King of France. To combat the royal forces the Camisards
had adopted a military organization. They were led by an
old soldier named only Rolland and Jean Cavalier, a former

baker's apprentice who the Camisards had come to believe was inspired by the Holy Spirit. The fanatical character of the revolt had been emphasized by the uncanny disregard of the Camisards for gunfire and death. Operating in a wooded, mountainous terrain which called for guerilla tactics, the Camisards had administered several sound drubbings to the royal army. The royal officials, headed by Intendant Bâville and Lieutenant General de Broglie (later by Marshal Montrevel), had attempted to suppress the revolt by the most cruel repression. In the single diocese of Mende 466 Protestant villages had been destroyed. In the diocese of Alais, Nîmes, and Uzès the incessant Camisard raids, the reprisals taken by the "volunteer" Catholic militia and the pillaging, murder, and arson on both sides brought devastation, terror, and death to a large portion of the population. For his part, Louis XIV found this religious revolt in his kingdom a steady drain on his already overtaxed military resources. The revolt became doubly serious when by the spring of 1704 two generals and 30,000 royal soldiers had proven incapable of crushing these peasants. The danger was ever present that the large Protestant population of the Midi might rise in revolt or that the allies might intervene there with material aid in the way of troops, arms, money, and munitions.[2]

[1] For expositions of the reasons for the Camisard revolt, see François André Isambert and others, *Recueil général des anciennes lois français depuis l'an 420 jusqu'à la révolution de 1789* (Paris, 1831-1833), XIX, 150, 160, 466, 492, 510, 520, 543, XX, 342; André Ducasse, *La guerre des Camisards* (Paris, 1946), 46-52; Abel Issarte, *Des causes de la révolte des Camisards* (Montbéliard, 1901), 67ff; Voltaire, *Le siècle de Louis XIV*, IIb, 184ff; Emile Léonard, *L'armée et ses problèmes au XVIIIe siècle* (Paris, 1956), 61; letter of Bâville to Chamillart in the *Bulletin de la société de l'histoire du Protestantisme français*, XXIV (1876), 136.

[2] Ducasse, *La guerre des Camisards*, 65ff, 71ff, 84-89, 116, 120ff, 150, 151ff; Léonard, *L'armée au XVIIIe siècle*, 71; Ernest Lavisse, *Histoire de France depuis les origines jusqu'à la révolution* (Paris, 1895), VIII, 381; Marcel Pin, *Jean Cavalier* (Nîmes, 1936), 134ff, 137, 142, 299; Agnes de la Gorce, *La guerre des Camisards* (Paris, 1950), 233; Claude de Vic and J. Vaisette, *Histoire générale de Languedoc*, ed. by Édouard Dulaurier and others, (Toulouse, 1872-1892), XIII, 799-801, for an excellent minute discussion of the

When the question of a commander for Languedoc became acute because of Marshal Montrevel's failure in the spring of 1704, Villars, still in disgrace, was without a command. The king charged his marshal with the repression of the Camisard Revolt. Fighting several hundred insurgents might seem a disgrace for the distinguished marshal of France, but successfully terminating the revolt would prove rewarding. Louis XIV stated to Villars that he would rather have this rebellion crushed than to win four major campaigns. Possibly he was not serious in this statement, but he did imply that Villars would be forgiven if the revolt was speedily terminated.[3]

Villars wished to regain the royal favor. Chamillart gave him the voluminous correspondence concerning the Camisard Revolt. Villars carefully digested these reports. He understood the situation and realized that his predecessors had ruined their reputations trying to suppress this revolt by force alone. He correctly reasoned that the complicity of the Cévenol peasantry enabled the Camisards to exist. Since the severest policies had failed, he decided to isolate the Camisards by appealing to the loyalty of the provincial upper classes, dispersing the atmosphere of fear among the peasants, and promoting a feeling of security among the "newly converted Catholics."[4] Villars also comprehended the necessity of curbing the excesses of the ecclesiastics and the Catholics. More than military talent would be needed to end this unhappy affair. After listening to arguments of all shades of the religious, political, and military spectrum,

destruction. *Mercure historique et politique,* XXXVI (January 1704), 92ff; Montrevel to Louis XIV, April 17, AG 1796, 82.

3 De Vogüé, *Mémoires,* II, 144ff; Dangeau, *Journal,* IX, 460, 461, 477.

4 The term "newly converted Catholics" refers to those who were Protestants before the revocation of the Edict of Nantes but who, since 1685, had accepted at least the outward forms of Catholicism; see *Mercure historique et politique,* XXXIII (January 1703), 66 and Voltaire, *Le siècle de Louis XIV,* IIb, 185.

Villars knew that he must impose his will on a hostile population.[5]

On his arrival in Nîmes on April 21 Villars declared that he would hang, shoot, or break on the wheel all those who were in a state of rebellion. But on the other hand to those who, within eight days, surrendered their arms he offered royal amnesty and the chance of leaving the country with their families and goods if they so desired. Hard-riding couriers carried his words into all parts of the province. Having given further notice of his intentions, Villars began to track down the Camisards. He formed several detachments of mixed cavalry and infantry of approximately 500 men each. These swift-moving forces were to march into the mountain wilderness using the six military roads in existence and then were to fan out in all directions to envelop the Camisard forces. On May 4 all was in readiness. At one precise moment 25,000 royal troops penetrated the mountain retreat of the Camisards. Pursued without rest and having no chance to descend to the lowlands for supplies, the Camisards fled to the thickest woods, to caves, and to camping areas so isolated as to be known only to them. But famine soon forced them from their hideouts. They ran into the now properly led royal troops, who cut them to ribbons on the open terrain. True to Villars' word, all those captured in a state of rebellion were killed.[6]

During this time Villars continued to tour the small villages of the province offering the olive branch to the hard-pressed Protestants. When he arrived in even the smallest

5 For Villars' attempts to arrive at the crux of the involved revolt and for a discussion of the Baron d'Aigaliers, his motives and influence on the "new Catholics," see Villars to Chamillart, May 13, June 23, AG 1796, and Bâville to Chamillart, April 12, AG 1796; the reports of interviews of Brigadier General Julien and Villars are recorded in Julien to Chamillart, March 28, AG 1796; Bâville to Julien, February 26, March 4, AG 1798; Chamillart to Montrevel, April 3, AG 1798.

6 *Mercure historique et politique*, XXXVI (April 1704), 432ff; Villars to Chamillart, April 20, AG 1796; Villars to Chamillart, May 9, AG 1796; for Villars' systematic troop dispositions see his report to Chamillart, AG 1796, 113, 114.

places he assembled the inhabitants, dismounted, and addressed them in the simple language that had proven so effective on privates of the line. Villars said that he was not ignorant of their sufferings and that he was attempting to bring the "time of troubles" to an end. He told them that the king did not like a revolt which had cost him 8,000 subjects in two years and tied down many of his best battalions when the Germans were victorious everywhere. Since his personal prestige and his glorious deeds were known to all, the simple peasants were filled with awe and respect for this marshal who talked to them on foot. And when the distinguished man in his white uniform covered with gold braid and decorations personally tore down a gallows while announcing that the terror was ended, they carried his honey-coated words to their relatives in the vastness of the mountains.[7]

Then, as the charm began to work and a few Camisards hesitatingly came in to lay down their arms, Villars publicly received them and, after giving them beautifully embossed letters of pardon, sent them home. And to give their friends, who might still fear a trick, time to consider Villars extended the period for amnesty to June 5. This extension of the time allotted, added to the stern, unrelenting tactics of the royal troops and the exhaustion of the Camisards, turned the tide. The first few to submit were counted by the dozen as small, isolated bands came in day by day. But, as long as Rolland and, especially, Cavalier remained at large, the stubborn backbone of the revolt remained unbroken.[8]

But flushed from their hiding place by hunger, the largest band of Camisards, led by Cavalier, fought a three-hour pitched battle on the heights of Nages. The dead on both sides numbered more than 400. After having two horses

[7] Villars to Chamillart, April 25, 27, May 11, AG 1796; *Mercure historique et politique*, XXXVI (May 1704), 561ff; Villars to Chamillart, May 2, AG 1796.
[8] Dangeau, *Journal*, X, 4, reports the news of thirty Camisards submitting as an occasion for great rejoicing at Versailles; Bâville to Chamillart, March 24, AG 1799.

shot from under him, Cavalier managed to regain the cover of the woods with the remnant of his band. Lieutenant General La Lande, however, gave the band no respite but followed so closely that he uncovered the caverns that contained the supplies and hospital of the Camisards.[9]

Cavalier meditated. The soldiers of the king now won the skirmishes and picked up the arms left on the battlefield. Marshal Villars' vigorous pursuit and offer of amnesty operated to undermine the loyalty of the Protestant peasantry, drying up the stream of recruits. The harvest was yet months away. Cavalier could divide his band into small groups that might escape detection, but what could replace the loss of equipment and martial spirit among his men? His lack of war material and recruits in May 1704 had been aggravated by a loss of morale.[10]

Cavalier claimed that the Holy Spirit advised him to discuss a general armistice with the royal officers. At a preliminary meeting with La Lande on May 12 he requested a personal interview with Marshal Villars. The exact words spoken at Pont d'Avesnes, their place of meeting, were known only to Cavalier and La Lande. When Cavalier returned to his band he ordered the men to list their imprisoned relatives, for all soon would be freed. The letter of submission that Cavalier signed demanded amnesty for all those of his religion, permission to leave the realm, and freedom for all those held prisoner for religious reasons.[11]

9 Bâville to Chamillart, April 28, AG 1799; Villars to Chamillart, April 28, AG 1796; Villars to Chamillart, May 4, AG 1796; *Mercure historique et politique*, XXXVI (May 1704), 555ff; Jean Cavalier, *Memoirs of the War of the Cévennes* (London, 1727), 233; Charles de La Baume, *Rélation historique de la révolte des fanatiques ou des Camisards* (Nîmes, 1794), 295, paints an excellent picture of the beginning of the military decline of power of the Camisards.

10 Cavalier, *Memoirs*, 222-27.

11 *Mercure historique et politique*, XXXVI (June 1704), 624ff; Cavalier, *Memoirs*, 260; La Baume, *Rélation historique*, 298; copy of the letter written by Cavalier to Villars in the presence of La Lande, May 13, AG 1796. See also Villars' letter to Louis XIV, May 13, AG 1796, and Cavalier, *Memoirs*, 260-63.

Villars was pleased that Cavalier did not ask for freedom of religion; and he assured Cavalier, during a personal interview in Nîmes, that the king would accept the Camisard's conditions. Inwardly Villars was happy because Cavalier's will to resist had obviously been broken by his own policy of amnesty and rigorous pursuit. The weaker of the Camisards were gradually accepting the offer of pardon. The more dedicated of the rebels were gradually being destroyed by the relentless pursuit of the royal troops. Villars had always believed in showmanship and intimidation. Here in the Cévennes he added an offer of amnesty to these two features. The combination was proving irresistible.

At Versailles Chamillart enthusiastically replied that His Majesty accepted the requests and prayers of Cavalier. Louis XIV personally wrote Villars a letter of congratulation. The king gave him the authority to sign all the necessary documents, free the prisoners, and care for the rebels.[12]

However the success or failure of Villars' method still depended a great deal on Cavalier's powers of persuasion. In the woods of Bouquet, Cavalier used all his eloquence to persuade his band to submit. He had not insisted on freedom of religious assembly because he knew that this could not be obtained except by decisive victories. Cavalier assured his followers that he would go to Holland, solicit aid, and recommence the revolt with a better chance of success. His discouraged and hungry Camisard followers accepted this solution.[13]

But all his powers of persuasion, threats, and "séances with God" could not sway Rolland. This leader continued to declare that he would lay down his arms only when liberty of conscience had been assured. By what right, Rolland wanted to know, had Cavalier surrendered all the Camisards.

[12] Chamillart to Bâville, May 18, AG 1799; Louis XIV to Villars, May 18, AG 1796. See also Dangeau, *Journal*, X, 15ff.
[13] Cavalier, *Memoirs*, 263; Villars to Chamillart, May 9, AG 1796; Bâville to Chamillart, May 9, AG 1799.

Perhaps he, Cavalier, had become a traitor to his religion. Humiliated and depressed, Cavalier marched to Nîmes and submitted to Villars with the few rebels who still followed him, but most of the band remained behind with Rolland.[14]

However, urged on by Villars, who still hoped for a lightning end to the revolt, Cavalier tried one last time. He arranged a meeting with Rolland at which he maintained that the king was indeed living up to his bargain. The relatives of those who had submitted were now free of imprisonment. He, Cavalier, would soon form a regiment to fight for the king to prove their loyalty to France. Would not the others still at large come in and end the losing battle before it was too late? Instead of agreeing, Rolland ran Cavalier and his party out of the Camisard camp at gunpoint. Cavalier had shifted his ground to compliance because he saw the futility of continued resistance when it was obvious that Villars would keep sufficient battalions in the field to destroy those who continued to resist. Villars, infuriated by this reverse, formed six strong units with orders to stay in the mountains until Rolland was captured or killed.[15]

For the rebels who remained under arms, the wilderness became more and more untenable. Every day they were hunted and gradually ground down under the weight of the 25,000 royal soldiers constantly in the field. Faced with ever-dwindling resources, Rolland split his band into small groups. For some time Rolland continued to elude the royal forces, but on August 14 a spy furnished Brigadier General Paratte, Villars' subordinate, with exact information on his whereabouts. The brigadier general thereupon surrounded the Castle of Castelnau at four o'clock in the morning. The

14 Villars to Chamillart, May 24, AG 1796; Bâville to Chamillart, June 5, AG 1799; De Vogüé, *Mémoires,* II, 153; Cavalier, *Memoirs,* 242; Devic and Vaisette, *Historie générale,* XIII, 840.

15 Cavalier to Bâville, May 29, AG 1799; Cavalier to Villars, May 29, AG 1796; De Vogüé, *Mémoires,* II, 312; La Lande to Chamillart, May 31, June 2, AG 1798; Bâville to Chamillart, June 11, AG 1799; Villars to Chamillart, June 11, AG 1796; Jacques Jacob de Kassel, baron d'Aigaliers, *Mémoires et lettres* (Paris, 1935), 55.

sleepy Camisard sentry gave the alarm too late. Rolland, who had come with only eight men to see his sweetheart, was awakened by the gunfire. He leaped from a window only to be tracked down and shot in the woods. Six of his band were taken prisoner. True to his word, Villars ordered all six to be broken on the wheel. They died displaying silent courage while praying for their tormentor.[16]

Deprived of their leaders, short of military supplies, starving, and demoralized, the Camisards moved toward complete submission. Villars permitted all who so desired to leave the country, but he continued the relentless pursuit. By September 20, 1704, 530 had surrendered. Of this number, only 130 chose to leave France. The king was informed on October 1, 1704, that the province was pacified. Most of the royal troops were immediately ordered elsewhere. Peace had come to a troubled province after a period of two years, but only five months after Villars had taken command.[17]

On December 4, 1704, Villars convened the Estates of Languedoc. He observed to Chamillart that no provincial parliament could be more majestic. He sat on an elevated throne, with the captain of the guard at his feet. To his right were three archbishops and twenty bishops representing the clergy; to his left, as members of the second estate, were the intendant, various lieutenants general, maréchaux de camp, commissioners of the king, and twenty-three nobles. Before the throne sat the deputies of the third estate. The parliament wildly acclaimed the marshal for ending the revolt and voted him a gift of 12,000 livres.[18]

During two years, from July 2, 1702, until September 30, 1704, a body of less than 2,000 peasants defied the power of Louis XIV. Successful in its earlier stages because of the

16 Bâville to Villars, October 10, AG 1799; Villars to Chamillart, October 11, AG 1797; *Mercure historique et politique*, XXXVII (October 1704), 432ff.

17 Bâville to Villars, October 10, AG 1799; Villars to Chamillart, October 11, AG 1797; Henri Carré, *Le maréchal Villars* (Paris, 1936), 105.

18 Villars to Chamillart, December 5, AG 1797; Villars to Chamillart, December 7, AG 1797; De Vogüé, *Mémoires du duc de Villars*, II, 167.

inability of the royal commanders, the revolt collapsed when faced with the sagacious Villars. He resorted to a combination of energetic pursuit with superior forces and conciliation. His policy of offering amnesty to those who would submit and death to those who continued defiant was the result of a careful analysis of the military, political, and religious fabric of the province of Languedoc. A basic understanding of the Camisard mentality and military organization enabled him to detach Cavalier and afterwards to crush Rolland.

Now that the province was peaceful, events in the War of the Spanish Succession forced Villars' recall from Languedoc. The Battle of Höchstädt-Blenheim on August 13, 1704, had ended in a complete rout for the French army of Marshal Tallard, placing France in a precarious position as Landau once again became an imperial possession. Her eastern frontier was now exposed to the armies of Eugene and Marlborough. Louis XIV once more turned to his most competent marshal. On January 6, 1706, the Duke of Berwick, natural son of the dethroned James II of England, assumed command in Languedoc. Villars returned to Versailles. To mark his return to royal favor Louis XIV elevated him to a dukedom and gave him command of the Army of the Rhine.[19]

Villars never apologized to the king for the actions that led to his disgrace in 1703. As a result he had learned nothing, and his arrogance in the near future would force the king again to relegate him to the minor theaters of war while a succession of incompetents would bring France close to military disaster in the Spanish Netherlands.

[19] Villars' last report to Chamillart, January 4, 1705, assured the court that the province was so peaceful that one might sleep throughout his passage. Devic and Vaisette, *Histoire générale de Languedoc*, XIV, 2007ff; *Mercure historique et politique*, XXXVIII (January 1705), 69; De Vogüé, *Mémoires du duc de Villars*, II, 160ff, 168; Carré, *Le maréchal Villars*, 107.

CHAPTER FIVE

Winning in a Losing War, 1705-1708

IN THE SPRING OF 1705 THERE SEEMED TO BE NO DOUBT that the imperial army, led by the House of Habsburg, in possession of Landau and free from all fear of French penetration into Germany, would attempt to invade the French province of Alsace from the north. Throughout the winter months the imperials had concentrated men and supplies in the vicinities of Trier and Koblenz. French scouting parties and outlying garrison commanders reported the Rhine full of barges bringing supplies of all kinds and reinforcements to these two points. The Duke of Marlborough was assembling an Anglo-Dutch army of 60,000 and counted on an additional 40,000 to march north under the command of the Prince of Baden. For the defense of this frontier Louis XIV had only 35,000 men.[1]

Ordered to take command of the Army of the Rhine on February 3, 1705, Villars began by reinforcing the garrisons in Saarlouis and Thionville. An unusually heavy rainfall that caused flooding over much of the countryside prevented both sides from actively engaging in the campaign before May.[2]

Villars wrote Chamillart on May 6 that he had learned that the Prince of Baden and the Duke of Marlborough were going to attack the Saar in a combined operation. If the king so wished he would fight a pitched battle. Louis XIV replied by ordering the *Maison du Roi* forces (household troops) and strong detachments from the armies of Alsace and Flanders to reinforce Villars. As a consequence Villars was able to move with a field army of 25,000 men on Sierck, with his advanced guard at Bouzonville, and his principal wings resting on Saarlouis and Thionville. After hurriedly entrenching and warning his men that should the enemy come there would be no quarter asked or given, he settled down to await the combined allied might opposed to him.[3] His Army of the Rhine was all that barred Marlborough's route to Paris.

While some social amenities were in process, Villars was stripping all cities and fortified places to his rear of every cannon, musket, and man fit for military duty. Still he had only 52,000 troops, including his dismounted cavalry, while his adversary had at least double that number. Chamillart advised him however that a reinforcement of fifteen battalions and twenty squadrons was on the march from the Army of Flanders.[4]

But these reinforcements could not possibly arrive before June 16, and Marlborough was making dispositions that led Villars to believe an attack imminent. The defending French army braced itself for what appeared to be an unequal contest when, on June 17, the Anglo-Dutch decamped and marched north. In a note to Villars, following the military custom of the age, Marlborough stated that the re-

1 Pelet, *Mémoires militaires*, V, 381ff; Josef Rechberger Ritter von Rechkorn, *Spanischer Successions-Kreig, Feldzug 1705* (Vienna, 1881), 288ff.

2 For Villars' preparations see AG 1851, 111ff, and AG 1852, 32-58.

3 Villars to Chamillart, May 6, 12, AG 1852; Marlborough to Harley, May 13, in John Murray (ed.), *The Letters and Dispatches of John Churchill . . . from 1702-1712* (London, 1845), II, 43; Louis XIV to Villars, May 14, AG 1852; Rechkorn, *Feldzug 1705*, 301. For the gradual reinforcement of Villars' position see AG 1852, 195-280.

4 The gross exaggerations of Marlborough's strength are in AG 1853, June 4-13.

fusal of the Prince of Baden to reinforce him left him no choice but to retire.[5]

Villars himself had very little to say about the event except to report that the Duke of Marlborough had done him the honor of suddenly marching away without attacking. Louis XIV was less cautious in his estimation of Marlborough's reasoning. He simply concluded that the sudden departure had been entirely due to the firmness of Villars. Other reasons have been given for what appeared to the French a sudden withdrawal of Marlborough. Perhaps the deeply entrenched and fervent French troops caused the Duke to consider that his losses might be out of all proportion to the advantage he would gain from forcing the lines. All previous historians have overlooked the fact that the Marshal Villeroi had begun a limited offensive in Flanders designed to relieve the allied pressure along the Moselle. The panic of the Dutch, so skillfully described by William Coxe and John W. Fortescue in their biographies of Marlborough, led to a decision that the Dutch units on the Moselle must return north. Marlborough did not find the Prince of Baden waiting for him; indeed, when Prince Louis did arrive, he brought only thirteen to fourteen thousand poorly equipped troops. Therefore Marlborough's retreat on the Moselle cannot be credited to any action of Villars. Marlborough simply did not have the men and supplies to defeat Villars and then march on Paris.[6] Actually the French Army of the Rhine outnumbered Marlborough's forces, but Villars never knew. He would have done well to have sent out scouting parties. This mistake is pardonable in light of

5 Villars to Louis XIV, June 17, AG 1853; Villars to Chamillart, June 17, AG 1853; Villars to Maintenon, in De Vogüé, Correspondance, I, 270ff.

6 The problem of why Marlborough withdrew has been dealt with by many scholars, but the above contention is drawn from AG 1853 (June 1704), especially 108, 109, 115; Murray, Correspondence, I, 569, 588ff, 601, II, 18ff, 21ff, 24ff, 33ff, 55, 58, 63ff, 69, 113; Villeroi to Villars, June 19, in De Vogüe, Mémoires, II, 249ff: William Coxe, Memoirs of John, Duke of Marlborough with Original Correspondence (London, 1818), I, 389-400; John W. Fortescue, Marlborough (London, 1932), 31ff.

Marlborough's reputation and the makeup of the units under Villars' command.

The Prince of Baden, who had failed properly to reinforce the Duke of Marlborough, was solidly entrenched on the Lauter and the heights of Wissembourg, from which positions he still menaced Alsace. Without abandoning his strong positions around Sierck, Villars decided to march for an attack on the hapless prince. He opened his campaign with a forced march on Trier. The imperial General Opach fled on June 24 with his garrison after dumping his supplies in the Moselle.[7]

The bulk of the French army arrived before the entrenchments of Wissembourg, held by 6,000 crack imperial troops, on July 4. True to his method of warfare, Villars entered the area in order of battle and, as soon as a battalion came into position, it was rushed at the double in a furious bayonet charge against the imperials. The first wave of the attacking French infantry breached the defenses, killing an estimated 1,500 of the enemy. Then Villars reformed his battalions and marched on the Castle of Sels and the fortress of Homburg. Both places fell as rapidly as did Wissembourg to the long lines of cheering French infantry. These victories were accomplished by such rapid marches that the Prince of Baden barely had time to break his camp at Schlangebad, much less to interfere.[8]

Moving with the extreme care customary in eighteenth-century warfare, the Prince of Baden marched his reserves into strongly fortified positions at Stolhoffen on August 1. Villars passed the Rhine in two columns, one at Kehl and the other at Gambsheim, and on August 12 launched a full-scale assault on the advanced posts which defended the Rhine. His cavalry roamed far and wide, burning and destroying

---

[7] Series of letters, Villars, Chamillart, Louis XIV, June 19-July 2, AG 1853.
[8] Villars, Marsin, Chamillart, July 4-28, AG 1845; Villars to Maintenon, July 4, in Charles Jean Melchoir, marquis de Vogüé, *Madame de Maintenon et le maréchal de Villars, correspondance inédite* (Paris, 1881), 23.

all that could not be carried away. War had indeed come to the Empire. The Prince of Baden remained behind his fortifications unaware that, with the threat to Alsace removed, all the reinforcements previously sent to Villars had been returned to their home stations.[9]

The frantic pleas for help on the part of the Prince of Baden, resulting from Villars' success, brought considerable reinforcements to the beleaguered imperial. Villars soon judged his own force far too inferior to attack Baden's principal line of fortifications. He consequently retreated behind the stream of Brompt and did not trouble the prince when the imperials marched to besiege Haguenau on August 20. Haguenau withstood the best efforts of the imperials until October 5; then the garrison, leaving behind 1,800 dead and wounded, pierced the enveloping siege lines to return in good order to Villars. In the meantime Villars struck at the imperial supply camp at Hochfelden, killing or capturing its entire garrison, and then forced the pass of Valkirk in the Black Mountains. At length, on September 1, orders came from Versailles forcing him to stand on the defensive.[10]

Shortly thereafter bad weather intervened to make further campaigning in the treacherous terrain impossible. Villars established his army in winter quarters behind the Bruche and returned to his general headquarters at Metz. In the season of 1705 he had not only witnessed the Duke of Marlborough's withdrawal but, with an apparently inexhaustible energy that seemed to infect his troops, had carried on a highly successful campaign on the farther side of the Rhine.

During the winter of 1705-1706 the Prince of Baden made up for his inactivity of the previous summer by establishing his forces on the Modder, reinforcing the garrison in Haguenau, driving in the outposts of Fort Louis, and fortifying

[9] Villars to Chamillart, July 29, 30, August 2, 12, 14, AG 1845, 1846; Dangeau, *Journal*, X, 386.
[10] Chamillart, Villars, Louis XIV, August 17-October 8, AG 1846.

his lines around Stolhoffen as far as Philippsburg. Villars, in the spring of 1706, conferred with Louis XIV on a new plan of campaign. They decided to chase the enemy from the Modder and to secure the approaches to Fort Louis. Villars, still in command of the Army of the Rhine, was to cooperate with Marshal Marsin who led the Army of the Moselle. Together they had eighty-eight battalions and 130 squadrons.[11]

On May 1 Villars moved his general headquarters to Strasbourg and, after his usual hasty but thorough reconnaissance, chose as his first objective the little place of Drusenheim. Marsin raised objections about the danger of the enterprise and declared that he would not order his troops into unfamiliar territory. Villars brushed aside his objections, saying that he would show him what he thought of such timidity. Accompanied only by 200 grenadiers and two squadrons of horse, Villars personally led assaults on all the small enemy strong points leading to his objective. When the impressionable imperials saw his standard they abandoned their fortifications after mere token resistance. On May 6 the governor of Drusenheim capitulated. Several days later the Castle of Haten fell to the assault, and the entrance to the Rhine bridge at Stattmatten was cleared. On May 10 the French appeared before Haguenau, which fell after a short siege of three days. In a period of thirteen days this remarkable marshal of France had taken 2,000 prisoners and fifty pieces of cannon with no more than a handful of men.[12]

[11] Marsin to Chamillart, April 24, AG 1948; Chamillart to Villars, April 25, AG 1948; Villars to Chamillart, April 27, 29, AG 1948; Emil Freiherrn Mayerhofen Grünbühl and Camille Freiherrn Komers von Lindenbach, *Spanischer Successions-Krieg, Feldzug 1706* (Vienna, 1882), 241-344.

[12] Villars to Chamillart, May 1, 7, 9, 11, AG 1948; Villars to Louis XIV, May 2, 4, 6, AG 1948; Marsin to Chamillart, May 5, AG 1948; Marsin to Villars, May 5, AG 1948; Villars to Maintenon, May 4, in Françoise d'Aubugné, marquise de Maintenon, *Lettres* (Amsterdam, 1756), VII, n.p.; Grünbühl and Lindenbach, *Feldzug 1706*, 344-53.

Pausing only long enough for the rest of the combined army to come up, Villars took swift advantage of his surprise attack. He marched to the Lauter, took over the old works of the Prince of Baden and solidly entrenched himself with his left at Wissembourg and his right on the Rhine near Lauterbourg. But Villars was, in principle, opposed to defensive tactics. He wrote Chamillart that French soldiers were never content to remain behind walls but asked only a chance to throw themselves upon the enemy. Villars sent parties of cavalry toward Koblenz and Mainz where they swept the imperial mounts from the countryside. After determining that no significant imperial force was to his rear between the Moselle and the Rhine, Villars proposed to lay siege to Landau. This would at least force the Prince of Baden to accept battle or lose a key fortress. But the grave defeat of Marshal Villeroi at Ramillies on May 23 necessitated that a strong reinforcement be sent to the Army of Flanders. On June 14 ten battalions started for the north and Villars had only fifty remaining. Then on June 22 Villars was ordered to replace Vendôme in Italy under the supreme command of the Duke of Orleans.[13] Marshal Vendôme had bungled in Italy, and the Duke of Orleans was clamoring for a command. Louis XIV needed a marshal to second the royal prince. Villars was available.

The prospect of commanding in the Italian theater did not suit Villars at all. He wrote Chamillart that if things were going badly in Italy he would go and see what he could do. But if possible, could not the king send Marsin instead? On the same day Villars wrote the king that he would be of far greater service in Germany than in Italy. Once again Louis XIV demonstrated great forbearance and replied that the change was necessary. Another exchange of letters followed and Marsin went to Italy. This time Louis XIV

13 Villars, Chamillart, Louis XIV, May 14-June 22, AG 1948.

obviously preferred Villars, services to another probable fiasco such as had occurred in 1703.[14] The king was approaching the realization that he could not do without Villars. While Louis XIV and the now-exiled Elector of Bavaria preferred Marsin on the Rhine because of the incidents in 1703, Louis would not spare his only competent marshal. It was still to be three years before the military position of France was desperate enough for Louis to gamble on placing Villars in command in the Spanish Netherlands, the area of greatest importance.

Villars did not remain inactive even though his army had been reduced. In preparation for an offensive on the other side of the Rhine he determined to drive the enemy from the island of Marquisat to relieve the pressure on Fort Louis. The island was separated from France by a branching of the Rhine and was uninhabited in time of peace. Under the cover of night twelve companies of grenadiers were led by Villars to a point on the bank opposite the main imperial fortification. At the break of day, under full view of the enemy garrison and without artillery cover, he ordered his men into boats, rowed across the Rhine and mastered the island. Villars wrote in his subsequent report that the grenadiers of Champagne and Navarre had faced the imperial fire in such a fashion as had been common in the days of the king's youth. On the very evening of this success Villars received orders to besiege Landau. Louis was desirous of diversionary action to relieve allied pressure in the Spanish Netherlands. If Villars had ever seriously considered this operation during the spring, he judged it quite risky now, especially since, by the last reports, the Prince of Baden had regained the field with double his number of effectives. The king bowed to his judgment.[15]

14 Villars, Chamillart, Louis XIV, June 27-July 1, AG 1948; Dangeau, *Journal*, XI, 138ff, 146; *Mercure historique et politique*, XLI (July 1707), 47.
15 Villars to Chamillart, July 11, 30, AG 1948; Chamillart to Louis XIV, July 17, AG 1948; Villars to Louis XIV, July 30, AG 1948; Dangeau, *Journal*, XI, 162.

Villars was concentrating his troops on the Lauter when, on September 13, he received the information, via an unknown secret agent, that the Prince of Baden was moving by forced marches to attack him. In fact, on the following morning the imperial standards were struck less than eight miles north of Wissembourg. After a short reconnaissance of the enemy positions, Villars confirmed his suspicion that he was outnumbered. But confident in the superior fighting qualities of his troops, he was preparing for battle when an order from Versailles ordered him to stand on the defensive. Marshal Villeroi had already had one army destroyed at Ramillies in May and, after the battle, Marlborough had driven the French back to a line just north of Lille. While Louis XIV might countenance a siege, he could hardly run the risk of a second rout. Characteristically Villars chose to consider the order as a personal insult. Thenceforth, from September 23 to November 24, when they left for winter quarters, the armies of the prince and the marshal sat and looked at each other—each waiting for the other to attack.[16]

In the spring of 1707 Villars' vigorous offensive on the right side of the Rhine gave Louis XIV time to repair his shattered Army of Flanders. Villars planned to force the defensive line on the right bank, which controlled the north passage through the Black Forest. Circumstances seemed favorable for such a hearty and difficult enterprise. The Prince of Baden had died and been replaced by the incompetent Margrave of Bareith. Villars was given sixty-six battalions, 108 squadrons and sixty-four pieces of cannon. But by May 1 the imperials had summoned fifty-seven battalions, sixty-nine squadrons and seventy-six cannon to oppose him from their solid entrenchments. Beginning on

[16] For the period between August 1 and September 12, when both sides were busily reequipping their units see AG 1949; Villars to Chamillart, September 13, 14, AG 1949; Chamillart to Villars, September 16, AG 1949; For the period September 23-November 24 see AG 1949; also see Grünbühl and Lindenbach, *Feldzug 1706*, 367-71.

the Rhine, at the head of a bridge defended by a small fort
on the island of Alunden, the imperial lines passed by the
village of Stolhoffen and extended into the neighboring low
hills of the burg of Biehl, itself strongly fortified. Along the
entire front of the line the fortifications were uninterrupted,
backed by numerous palisaded redoubts and seconded in
large part by a system of inundation devised by Dutch engineers. Villars decided to bring about the fall of this
seemingly impregnable position by the following tactics:
draw the attention of the imperials to their right flank by
two false attacks near the island of Alunden, while sneaking
a third force around the other flank to take the position in
the rear.[17]

During the night of May 20, 1707, a bridge of boats was
quietly thrown across the Rhine, and twenty battalions
crossed to the right bank. While these preparations were
going on Villars gave a brilliant military ball in Strasbourg
to allay suspicion and to ensure the continued tranquility of
the imperials. During the course of the ball Villars and his
general officers mounted and rode throughout the night to
reach Kehl early the next morning. The attack was sched-
uled for daybreak on May 22. At exactly 6 A.M. ten battalions
of the French line, making enough noise for fifty, attracted
the attention of the imperials on the island of Alunden by a
slow-step attack aided by the cannon of Fort Louis. When
the return fire disclosed that the engagement had become
general and that the imperials were concentrating on the
diversionary force, Villars led his third column around the
fortified line. So occupied were the defenders with what
they assumed to be a frontal assault that the French infantry penetrated the lines from the rear. When a thick
fog finally dispersed, on May 23, the imperials were found

---

[17] Chamillart to Cheyladet, February 11, AG 2027; Villars to Chamillart,
May 8, 11, 16, 20, AG 2027; Carl Freiherrn von Hipssich and Camille Frei-
herrn Komers von Lindenbach, *Spanischer Successions-Krieg, Feldzug 1707*
(Vienna, 1883), 204-208.

to have decamped. By midmorning the French were in possession of the fortifications with very slight casualties.[18]

As was his custom, Villars began to exploit the success without the least hesitation. On May 24, while his cavalry finished taking possession of the remaining Rhine bridges, he entered Rastatt with his main forces. The Margrave of Bareith was stationed in Pforzheim with thirty-six battalions and seventy squadrons but quickly decamped at the first sight of the French. Villars occupied Pforzheim on May 28 and pushed on to Stuttgart where he learned that the imperials had stopped in Schorndorf, ten miles on the other side of the Neckar River. On June 15 the French army crossed the Neckar and appeared before Schorndorf.[19]

At this point Villars hesitated. He had only four siege guns with less than a hundred rounds each, and the fortress commandant appeared ready to resist. But, faithful to his principle of intimidation, Villars opened a trench that same evening. Two days later he informed the governor that unless he capitulated he would put the garrison and the entire population to the sword. The next day Schorndorf capitulated and Villars had fifty additional cannon.[20]

On the same day that Schorndorf fell, Villars was informed that the imperial rearguard (consisting of 5,000 men under Lieutenant General Janus) was solidly entrenched in three lines at the mouth of the gorge of Lorch. Villars launched a frontal assault. Despite an energetic defense with large losses on both sides, Janus was wounded and taken prisoner with some 600 men. Pushing ahead, Villars accepted the keys to Schwäbisch Gmünd on June 22.[21]

18 Villars, Chamillart, Pery, Quincy, May 23, AG 2027; Dangeau, *Journal*, XI, 376ff; Hipssich and Lindenbach, *Feldzug 1707*, 210ff.

19 Villars to Chamillart and Louis XIV, May 24-June 15, AG 2027; Dangeau, *Journal*, XI, 379ff, 387, 389ff, 393; Hipssich and Lindenbach, *Feldzug 1707*, 216ff.

20 Villars to Louis XIV, June 16, AG 2027; Dangeau, *Journal*, XI, 400ff; Hipssich and Lindenbach, *Feldzug 1707*, 218.

21 Villars to Chamillart, June 21, 23, AG 2027; Frémont to Chamillart, June 21, AG 2027; Villars to Louis XIV, June 22, AG 2027; Hipssich and Lindenbach, *Feldzug 1707*, 219.

All of Germany was in great consternation. There could be no doubt of Villars' intention to attack Vienna. The imperial war council feared that this marshal, with greater audacity than troops and military supplies, might try to restore the estates of the Elector of Bavaria and then to march on the heart of the Empire. At Versailles, despite his successes, there was an increasing uneasiness over Villars. Louis XIV expressed fear for the fate of an army that he could ill afford to lose if it continued to march deeper and deeper into the Empire. Quickly writing on June 23, he ordered Villars to besiege Heilbronn in order that his line of communication would never be in doubt.[22]

Also, in Vienna, Prince Eugene, but lately returned from Italy, estimated that the simplest way to remove Villars from Germany would be to collect the imperial troops that he had bypassed into a striking force. This calculation was correct. The imperial army, now under the command of the Elector of Hanover, augmented by 10,000 reinforcements, marched with all possible speed for the Rhine. Villars was forced to retreat in his own footsteps. Every foot of the way back was contested by small parties of imperials. At Dourlach he lost 300 men in a hotly contested skirmish. He covered 150 miles in six days to regain Philippsburg, where he blockaded the imperial army in that city.[23]

Villars had not surrendered the initiative to the imperials. He wrote the king that if the enemy maintained himself in Philippsburg, he would besiege the city. The imperials were intimidated and in great distress from too many forced marches. But for all his plans Villars found that his force was diminished when eight battalions were sent to Provence, where the Duke of Savoy had broken through the frontier defenses. Villars could not now force the imperials from

22 Louis XIV to Villars, June 23, AG 2027; Pelet, *Mémoires militaires*, VII, 214; Hipssich and Lindenbach, *Feldzug 1707*, 221.
23 Villars, Louis XIV, Chamillart, July 5, AG 2027; Hipssich and Lindenbach, *Feldzug 1707*, 222-26.

Philippsburg, nor had he sufficient equipment to pursue
a successful siege. So he departed and in a series of rapid
marches temporarily occupied Heidelberg on July 11, Mannheim on July 16, and finally camped at Ratstatt on August
30 to collect contributions and maintain his communications with France by the bridges of Neuburg and Kehl and
a newly established pontoon bridge at Ratstatt.[24]

During the course of the campaign of 1707 Villars again
had not been able to penetrate the heart of Habsburg power,
but his cavalry had swept into Franconia and Swabia and
Lieutenant General de Broglie had taken Ulm. Villars had
systematically imposed a system of forced contributions to
the French army. For example, as a result of treaties with
local authorities, Württemburg paid him 2,200,000 gold
livres, Baden 330,000, and even the small city of Schwäbisch
Gmünd 15,000. This did not include the large quantities
of grain, horses, munitions, and other supplies consumed by
his army or shipped back to France.[25] Villars wrote Chamillart that the German campaign did not cost the king a
sou but was a paying enterprise. This practice of collecting
contributions, while actually little more than thinly disguised looting, was part of the accepted standards of warfare
during the old regime. Certainly Louis XIV approved.
Chamillart wrote that the king was thankful for the several
millions he had received. Despite the large amounts of gold
flowing into his coffers from Villars' enforced levies on the
occupied part of Germany, Louis XIV did not consider that
the general war situation would permit the Army of the
Rhine to winter in Germany. Hence Villars received orders
to enter winter quarters on the French bank of the Rhine.
On November 11 he returned to Versailles.[26]

24 Villars, Louis XIV, July 7-September 2, AG 2027, 2028; Hipssich and
Lindenbach, *Feldzug 1707*, 227ff.

25 For the story of this thinly disguised looting see AG 2027, 97-231, AG
2028, 2-65.

26 Villars to Chamillart, August 11, AG 2028; Louis XIV to Villars, May
28, AG 2027; Chamillart to Villars, July 13, October 19, AG 2027, 2028.

While Villars' campaigns in 1705, 1706, and 1707 had been successful, this was not the case with the other armies of the king. In fact on all other fronts the reverse had been true. In Spain the imperials had driven Philip V from Madrid, and all attempts to retake Gibraltar from the English failed. In the north the disaster at Ramillies (1706), where Villeroi had badly bungled, gave the allies command of most of the Spanish Netherlands. In Piedmont the inability of La Feuillade had cost the French Turin, all the Milanese, and even part of the French Alps. In 1707 Prince Eugene had penetrated Provence and besieged Toulon while the English shelled the city from the sea. Fortunately Toulon held out.

It was to this theater of war in the southeast that Villars once more was ordered. Although he again complained of having to leave his Army of the Rhine, this time there was no reprieve from the order of Louis XIV. At the moment when he started south Prince Eugene was recalled and sent to Flanders. The Duke of Savoy, Victor Amédée, had concentrated his troops in Savoy and Piedmont for a penetration of Dauphiné. Reinforced by the Austrians, Victor Amédée had an army of fifty-six battalions and 10,000 cavalry while Villars did not have half that number to patrol and hold the 300 miles from Geneva to the sea.[27]

When the marshal arrived at Grenoble on June 8, 1708, his first need was to make a tour of inspection. While doing this, Villars ordered his commandants to maintain their positions as long as a man lived. However, he confided that he did not feel at ease in the high, mountainous terrain so different from the Rhineland.[28]

After centering his mobile force on Chambéry in early July, Villars was startled by the news on the twentieth that

27 Louis XIV to Villars, April 28, May 2, AG 2091, 2099; Villars to Chamillart, May 14, AG 2091; Chamillart to Villars, May 31, AG 2099.
28 Villars to Chamillart, June 3, 18, 22, AG 2099; comte de Muret to Chamillart, June 16, AG 2099; general disposition of troops on the frontier of Piedmont, AG 2099, 211.

the French entrenchments guarding the Little Saint Bernard Pass had been overrun by the superior forces of the Duke of Savoy. He quickly marched with all the troops he could collect, but the Duke of Savoy had countermarched, passed the bottleneck of Saint-Genève and marched on Briancon, which was held by a very weak garrison. Recognizing an exploit that smacked of his own audacity, Villars put his battalions by forced marches on the road to Galibier, a route held impassable for large bodies of troops. At the price of tremendous exertion the army climbed to the summit, losing men and equipment at every hairpin turn. Descending into the valley of Guissance, the French infantry reached the gates of Briançon on August 9, before Victor Amédée could effectively blockade the city.[29]

Undaunted, the Duke of Savoy marched on the Fortress of Exiles, which was situated on a high, easily defensible position and had a large garrison. But the commander capitulated almost at the first sound of the Savoyard cannon on August 14. Encouraged, Victor Amédée laid siege to Fenestrelle, another position considered impregnable. Villars sent an emissary to its governor with an order to hold out until a relieving column could arrive. But on August 20 the governor, De Barrière, signed a capitulation under threat of mutiny by his senior officers. Enraged, Villars wrote that those of this mind had best stay in the jails of Savoy for he would show them no mercy when they returned to France. Sending for the governors of Briançon, Château-Quétreas, Mont-Dauphin, and Embrun, he gave them strict instructions on how to repair their fortifications and offered them the choice between resigning or dying at their posts. But snow began falling in the very high mountains and made further operations impossible. The infuriated marshal then returned to Versailles.[30]

29 Villars, Artagnan, July 20, August 2, 9, AG 2100; Alexander Kirckhammer, *Spanischer Successions-Krieg, Feldzug 1708* (Vienna, 1885), 164-75.
30 Villars, Chamillart, August 12-September 2, AG 2100, 2101.

Once at Versailles, Villars pressed the king to hold a council of war on the conduct of the governors of Exiles and Fenestrelle. He wanted to make examples of them to encourage all the faint of heart. He reminded Louis XIV that a royal decree in 1705 stated that no governor should surrender a fortress until reduced to the last extremity. The officers responsible for the loss of the two towns were thereupon sentenced to perpetual imprisonment and confiscation of all their possessions. Such was the severity which Villars handed out to those he considered incompetent.[31]

But while Villars arrested the allied assault in the southeast, the Army of Flanders, commanded by the Duke of Burgundy and Marshal Vendôme, suffered a grave defeat at Audenaire that brought about the fall of Lille. The season of 1708 closed with the allies entrenched in French Flanders waiting only for the coming of the spring to penetrate to the very heart of France.

The campaigns of 1702-1708, when Villars commanded on secondary fronts reveal his personality in his attitude toward subordinates and superiors. The most important relationships of any general are with his fellow officers and his enlisted men. The enlisted men, in a word, loved Villars. He was the only winning general the French had. No soldier prefers to run away or to retreat constantly, year after year, or to be defeated, time and time again, because of incompetence at the top. The enlisted men adored Villars also for his willingness to share their hardships, for his good humor, and for his basic honesty. Villars had that relationship with his enlisted men that Napoleon, Caesar, and George Patton had. This magnetic relationship can be described in two words—mutual confidence.

For the officers it was somewhat otherwise. Villars' officers must have constantly verged on the edge of insanity. True, Villars did not demand anything of his officers that he had

31 Catinat, *Mémoires*, I, 346ff; De Vogüé, *Mémoires*, III, 31.

not already done himself. But the demands of death at one's post, no quarter for the enemy, no sacking of conquered cities, and disregard of enemy fire were often carried to the extreme. Therefore it is not surprising that Villars' subordinate officers either hated or loved him. The officers who informed on Villars in the 1703 Bavarian campaign and those prosecuted for incompetence in 1708 are examples of those who hated him. Villars' attitude toward his subordinate officers must have been something like this. If they were competent and carried out every order with a satisfactory spark of initiative, they had his favor. But should they show the slightest hesitation, especially under fire, or attempt to win favor by a courtier's methods, they risked his displeasure. To his senior officers Villars showed nothing but contempt. No matter how he might laugh with Boufflers or Vendôme, he always believed that he was the only competent marshal and made little or no attempt to hide his feelings.

Villars treated Louis XIV, Chamillart, Voisin, and Madame de Maintenon in much the same way as he did his subordinate officers. It is somewhat close to miraculous that Villars survived long enough to become a *maréchal de France*. Letters of the type cited in earlier chapters would have sent many Frenchmen to the block or life imprisonment. Saying "no" to a direct order of the king was more than most men ever dreamed of doing. It is no wonder that the court was shocked at the events of nearly every year. What then was Villars' personality? What quality did he have that enabled him to stop the rout at Freidlingen in 1702, to win at Höchstädt in 1703, to curb the Camisards in 1704, to defeat the imperials in 1705-1707, and to save the southeastern frontier in 1708? Five traits of his character have been uncovered so far—conceit, ability, volatile temper, acidity, and exhibitionism.

Villars' principles of warfare were directly related to his

personality. The only discernible constant of this man was his obsession to find the enemy and defeat him. Villars always believed that he could defeat an enemy who had far superior forces if he could trick him into committing a blunder. Once the enemy was on the field offering battle, Villars must charge into the thick of the fighting and by personal example lead his troops to victory (as at Freidlingen). When badly outnumbered and without supplies (as in 1705), he would go into the ground like a fox directly in the enemy's path and have to be dug out, at the cost of one soldier for five. At times he would use caution. Villars was careful and diplomatic in his handling of the Camisards. In the fall of 1705, 1706, and in 1707, he likewise displayed caution by retreating without giving battle.

Showmanship was an outstanding quality of Villars' character. Soldiers usually are proud of the general who is decorated for their labors, because they have shared in the making of the decoration and know the general's true worth. Villars' men were proud of him both at Freidlingen and in May of 1706.

Intimidation was a weapon that Villars constantly employed. But he was always serious when he threatened to sack a town or to put an entire population to the sword unless capitulation was immediately forthcoming. Villars probably did not ever say *"La Guerre c'est l'enfer,"* but he practiced the principle as surely as did Attila the Hun or William Tecumseh Sherman.

It is no wonder that Louis XIV was hesitant to employ such a man in the all-important Flemish theater of war. Here was a man who once defied the monarch and often demanded his own way to a fault but who had the knack of winning when all other marshals were losing. He might carry through to victory, but his impetuosity also was fraught with risk.

CHAPTER SIX

The Bootless Army of Malplaquet, 1709

THE YEAR 1709, ONE OF THE MOST TRAGIC IN THE HISTORY of France, opened amid famine and military defeat. With most of Vauban's fortress system in the hands of the allies, the Dutch dragoons swept as far south as the environs of Paris, attacking the garrison on the Pont de Sèvres. And while the entire realm suffered from want of even the bare necessities of life, the French army of Flanders, wintering in the few fortresses still left to Louis XIV and in the villages of Flanders, Artois, Hainault, and Picardy, deteriorated. Fénelon, the great Archbishop of Cambrai, wrote that Louis XIV, were he in town, would notice the lack of money on all sides. The garrison was not even being paid. He would see the discouragement of the army, the disgraceful actions of the officers, the misgovernment of the people, the ascendancy of the enemy, the silence of the people, and the irresolution of generals who feared to risk any enterprise. The archbishop went on to say that discipline, order, affection, and spirit had gone out of the army; in fact, all the old qualities had gone from France and would not return until the accursed war had ended.[1]

As the future would prove, Louis XIV did not suffer from

a lack of will power, nor did he desire peace without victory. Despite the difficulties of weather and shortage of supplies, the king decided upon a winter campaign to retake Lille and assigned the task to the aged Marshal Boufflers. Although Boufflers rejoined the Army of Flanders in its winter quarters, this old man of war was unable to cope with the enormous problems confronting him—no money to pay the soldiers; many men without overcoats and boots; some companies without a single serviceable fusil; some soldiers trading equipment for bread. What was more shocking, all the frustrations of a losing war and a starving time had bubbled over in the garrisons of Quesnoy, Arras, Mons, St. Omer, Tournai, Nassau, Valenciennes, and Cambrai, which mutinied and committed acts of violence against the local officials and townsmen.[2]

Perhaps the true logistical position of the Army of Flanders was stated by Intendant Bernières when he wrote that famine ruled the land. As officials tried to prepare for the winter campaign conditions only worsened. The magazines of war continued empty; money was not forthcoming; and the few officers who bothered to report for duty had not a single sou for their subsistence. The war contractors would not deliver supplies to the army even at usurious rates for fear of the civilians attacking their wagons.[3]

Into this terrible situation came the sixty-five-year-old Marshal Boufflers. Despite the privation and terrible weather (known in French history as the "Great Winter"), Boufflers went on a tour of inspection in an attempt to bolster the sagging morale of the French army. But the hardships broke

---

[1] Fénelon's description of the conditions during 1709 occurs in the essays, "Portrait de l'electeur de Baviere" and "Troisième mémoire sur la guerre de la succession d'Espagne" in *Oeuvres complètes de Fénelon* (Toulouse, 1810), IV, 107ff, and 57-79 respectively.

[2] *Mercure historique et politique*, XLVI (January 1709), 91-119; Eugene to the Emperor, January 3, in Josef Ritter Rechberger, *Spanischer Succession-Krieg, Feldzug 1709* (Vienna, 1886), #2; AG 2149, 249-54, 256, 258.

[3] Bernières to Chamillart, Nodot, Artois, February 9, AG 2154.

Bouffler's health, and from Arras he wrote, on February 21, that he could not carry on. At the end of March Marshal Boufflers was returned to Paris on a stretcher.[4]

The sickness of Boufflers and the terrible conditions not only in the army but throughout France forced Louis XIV to give command of the all-important Flanders theater of operations to Marshal Villars. This was a decision that the king had refused to make in the past because of Villars' seeming recklessness. It would be one thing for the audacity of Villars to lose fifty battalions in Germany but quite another for him to lose two hundred in Flanders. Villars did not adhere to the slow, painstaking methods common to the other marshals. This taint of rashness, when added to Villars' stubborn tendency for independent action, left a seed of doubt in the mind of Louis XIV. But in 1709 there was no one else. All the other marshals had failed to contain the Marlborough-Eugene combination, and besides the king no longer had 200 battalions for Flanders. Villars was appointed to command the Army of Flanders simply because there was no one else of competence available.

It had been fifteen years since Villars had been in Flanders, and his first action after arriving at Cambrai on March 18 was to visit all the king's camps on the frontier. Reports cascaded into Chamillart's office stating that nothing had been prepared or organized. The garrisons along the frontier were having difficulty in finding bread from day to day, much less storing sacks of grain for a campaign. However, Villars found the troops in better spirits than he had anticipated. For, in truth, the misery of the lands surrounding the winter quarters was so much worse that there had been few desertions. And if the officers of his general staff complained of their suffering, muttering that another campaign was impossible, the lower ranks of the officers displayed a

4 Boufflers to Louis XIV, February 21, AG 2149.

type of stoicism which Villars believed had not been seen since the days of Marcus Aurelius. When reporting on the professionals, Villars saw that they were remaining calm and loyal in their adversity as was the proper spirit of their trade. But the marshal wrote that their sufferings tore his heart. In such conditions he could not, in fact dared not, undertake the siege of Lille against an allied army—fat, sleek, and very numerous after a well-fed winter.[5]

Instead, Villars concentrated his energies in berating the minister of war. He also wrote to Madame de Maintenon and Louis XIV. But the suffering, lack of clothing, usable small arms, powder, horses, cannon, food, and forage had far less effect upon the court of the Sun Monarch than did the fact that the Duke of Marlborough and Prince Eugene were, without any attempt to disguise their movements, concentrating 180 battalions and 290 squadrons, at full strength, well supplied with money, supplies, and artillery. The allies openly boasted that the French army no longer knew how to fight and that 1709 would see the flags of the Empire, Holland, and England flying over Versailles.[6]

The extremity to which the Army of Flanders was reduced and the inability of the central government to overcome the supply problems led Villars to request a personal audience with Louis XIV. Leaving the frontier on May 9 and riding all night, Villars arrived at Chamillart's door just as the minister was getting out of bed. Leaping across the room at the startled marquis, Villars cried with vehemence, "You are the Secretary of War. Do you not realize that you are exposing yourself to horrible reproaches if you do not supply me. . . ? How is it that we do not have even boots and bread . . . that our weapons are unserviceable?"

5 Chamillart to Villars, March 14, AG 2150; Villars to Chamillart, Louis XIV, March 18, 20, 21, 28, AG 2150; state of the garrisons inspected by Villars, April 31, AG 2150.

6 Villars to Chamillart, March 18-April 10, AG 2150; Villars to Louis XIV, March 26, AG 2150; Chamillart to Villars, March 18-April 25, AG 2150.

Extremely annoyed at this outburst, Chamillart simply shrugged his shoulders and had the infuriated marshal shown into the hall.[7]

On the eleventh of May, Louis XIV held his weekly council of state at Marly with Villars in attendance. After the main council had finished its order of business, the king closeted himself with Chamillart, Desmartes, Marshals Harcourt, Boufflers, and Villars. Villars, obviously forgetting, or more likely tossing aside, any semblance of etiquette, leaped to his feet and began pounding the table in front of a very startled monarch as he revealed the condition of the Army of Flanders. Louis XIV agreed to ship 18,000 sacks of grain to Arras but then indicated that he could offer no other assistance. Turning to Villars, the now somewhat less than lustrous Sun King said, "All I have left is my confidence in God and you, my outspoken friend."[8]

When Villars returned to Arras three days later, the promised grain had not arrived. Since the central administration had obviously failed, Villars took matters into his own hands by sending his cavalry on a long sweep through Picardy, Soissonnais, Normandy, and Champagne with orders to seize all supplies needed by the army. Next, this man of war turned on the civilian contractors who would not furnish supplies without prompt payment in gold. He broke into their warehouses, confiscated everything, and kept them under guard with the army to silence their complaining tongues.[9]

By these illegal methods Villars had a two weeks' grain supply by May 31. The presence of bread more than any other item rallied the bootless, starving Army of Flanders.

[7] Villars to Chamillart, April 24, AG 2150; Chamillart to Villars, May 1, AG 2150; Villars to Louis XIV, May 4, AG 2150; Louis XIV to Villars, May 5, AG 2150; Villars to Maintenon, June 17, in De Vogüé, *Correspondance*, I, 333ff.

[8] Villars to Chamillart, May 11, AG 2150; Dangeau, *Journal*, XII, 412ff.

[9] Villars to Chamillart, May 15, 18, 19, AG 2150; Salian to Chamillart, May 15, AG 2150; Chamillart to Villars, May 17, AG 2150.

Slowly but surely the army was pulling itself together, becoming a force capable of disputing the soil of France with the allies. Villars' energy, but even more his tangible results, were contagious. By the end of May the opposing army, much to its amazement, saw a small but spirited French army march onto the field and dare its far more numerous adversary to attack. A miracle? Perhaps, but Villars' military skill and optimistic personality were the real answer. The marshal's methods were certainly not pleasant or morally correct. But they were necessary.[10]

The peace negotiations that had been conducted at The Hague throughout the winter of 1708-1709 were now interrupted as the ground thawed and an active campaign was possible. Knowing the terrible conditions within France and attempting to ensure that Louis XIV and his heirs would never again threaten the domination of Europe, the allies had demanded not only that France give up Alsace and her holdings in Lorraine but also that Louis XIV should declare war against his grandson, Philip V of Spain. To this last demand Louis XIV would not agree. The Marquis of Torcy, French plenipotentiary, stopped at Arras on his way back from The Hague to acquaint Villars with the results of the negotiations. The marshal wrote Louis XIV that such conditions were impossible and that the Army of Flanders would dispute every inch of French territory and decimate the enemy's battalions until he was sick and tired of the slaughter and the general revulsion of his population forced him from the war. On the second day of Torcy's visit, Villars drew up the thirty battalions of his line and, after informing them of the conditions that the allies sought to impose on their king, added, "Soldiers, the only hope of the king for an honorable peace rests on your bayonets. Al-

---

[10] Villars to Chamillart, May 22, 23, AG 2150; Chamillart to Villars, May 22, AG 2150; Louis XIV to Villars, May 27, AG 2150; Villars to Maintenon, May 24, Maintenon to Villars, May 26, in De Vogüé, *Correspondance*, I, 323, 324ff.

though we are outnumbered four to one we will ask no quarter and give none." To this passionate speech, the troops replied, "Vive le roi, vive le Maréchal." The very impressed Marquis of Torcy continued on his way to Versailles.[11]

The weary and battered Chamillart had been replaced. The able Daniel Voisin had been given the post of Secretary of War. But no administrator could cope with the impossible situation of the French army in the War of the Spanish Succession. Only reforms which were never to come could have alleviated the situation. Without any resources at all, Voisin wrote Villars that he would forward money and materials as they became available. Meanwhile, the marshal was to defend France. Such a letter, which was tantamount to *a carte blanche,* was very much to Villars' liking.[12]

On May 27 the forty battalions of the French field army camped before Lens. With only a few pieces of artillery to the allies' two hundred, Arras as the only reasonably secure supply point and most of the officers on foot, Villars faced the largest and best-equipped enemy army ever to threaten northern France in the War of the Spanish Succession. Furthermore, as is the habit of such people, the officers of the general staff constantly complained and eagerly discussed the good old days of siege warfare, seemingly oblivious to the privations of their men.[13]

Villars wrote to the king asking that several princes of the blood journey to the army to give the example by sharing the privations of the common soldiers. Here, however, he touched a very sensitive chord in the character of Louis

11 Chamillart to Villars, April 27, AG 2150; Villars to Torcy, April 15, 21, in De Vogüé, *Mémoires,* II, 246ff, 247ff; Villars to Louis XIV, June 1, 6, AG 2151.

12 Louis XIV to Chamillart, May 23, AG 2150; Voisin to Villars, June 10, 11, AG 2151.

13 Villars to Chamillart, May 27, 30, AG 2150; Villars to Louis XIV, May 29, AG 2150; Louis XIV to Villars, May 31, AG 2150.

XIV. The king had given the Duke of Burgundy command of the Army of Flanders in 1708 with catastrophic results. Louis placated Villars by saying that he had asked others and that no one wanted to come. But while the Bourbon blood stayed at Versailles, the pretender James III of England, serving under the pseudonym of the Knight of Saint George, rode up to offer his services. Madame de Maintenon informed Villars that the knight genuinely desired to be of service. But in the end it was the example of Villars, who seemed to face the might of the allies with resignation yet honor, that slowly revived the drooping spirits of the French general staff. On June 13 Villars was able to write that the talk of defeat and death had for the most part been silenced.[14]

By the middle of June the army was forced to accept daily delivery of its bread from Arras and on more than one day no bread arrived. Villars wrote, "There was no bread to give the men today. I am humble when I see the backbreaking labor the men perform without food."[15] Undoubtedly drawing some of his strength from his men, who in turn were getting theirs from his example, Villars refused to retire, as the king advised, behind the Scarpe. Instead the marshal entrenched between the Scarpe and the Lys with his right resting at Douai and his left at Béthune. From Douai to Pont-à-Mendin his position was protected by the Douai canal and impenetrable woods. In front of the center Villars constructed enormously strong field fortifications and a series of infantry trenches at thirty-foot intervals. Between Béthune and Saint-Venant he covered the left flank with field emplacements and made the slight elevation of Hensies into a veritable hornet's nest of cannon and sharpshooters. Installed in this manner, Villars hoped to resist a siege of Douai and to take by flank any army which

---

14 Villars to Voisin, June 13, 19, 21, AG 2151; Villars to Maintenon, June 25, in De Vogüé, *Maintenon et Villars*, 47ff.
15 Villars to Maintenon, June 6, in De Vogüé, *Maintenon et Villars*, 43ff.

tried to go between Aire and Saint-Omer. He thought that
the allies would have no choice but to assault his positions.[16]

But on June 21 he learned that Eugene and Marlborough
had concentrated their army between the Lys and the
Escault—obviously threatening Tournai. Even if the garrison of Tournai was short of food, it had plenty of munitions and a strong fortress. Sûrville, the energetic governor,
quickly confiscated the needed supplies for the garrison,
leaving the civilians to shift for themselves. Villars was de-
lighted when the allies began to invest Tournai. Every
battalion decimated before the walls of the fortress would be
one less he would have to fight.[17]

The preoccupation of the allies with Tournai left Villars
free for harassing actions. Writing that fortifications reduced the ardor of his troops and that they were not suited
for the French temperament, Villars announced the defeat
of a small enemy force attempting to fortify Warenton on
July 4. Some fifteen battalions under Lieutenant General
Artagnan surprised the allied garrison in a dawn attack. All
who attempted resistance were shot and some 700 prisoners
were taken before the allied army had time to dispatch reinforcements. This minor success caused the allies to increase
the size of their army of observation and therefore prolonged
the siege of Tournai.[18]

Knowing that he could count on a long and spirited
resistance from Tournai, Villars judged it safe to extend
his line of fortifications to the right. The French army occupied new positions between Helesme and Denain, with
the left flank secured by dense woods running along the

16 AG 2151, 12-82; Marlborough to Boyle, June 20, in Murray, *Correspondence*, IV, 510.
17 AG 2151, 87-126; Maintenon to Villars, June 30, in De Vogüé, *Correspondance*, I, 337ff; Eugene to the Emperor, June 26, 30, in Rechberger,
Feldzug 1709, #109, #113; Marlborough to Boyle, June 27, July 1, in Murray,
Correspondence, IV, 520, 522ff.
18 Villars, Sûrville, Louis XIV, July 1-5, AG 2151; Marlborough to Boyle,
July 8, in Murray, *Correspondence*, IV, 536; Eugene to the Emperor, July
3, 6, in Rechberger, *Feldzug 1709*, #119, #128.

bank of the Scarpe and the right flank on the Escault. In this way the marshal could effectively oppose the investiture of Condé or Valenciennes.[19]

The material situation continued to cause Villars grave concern. During the winter the soldiers had not been paid, and only half their current wages was forthcoming. The problem of provisioning remained unsolved. Villars wrote that he had no bread to give his soldiers every third day but that their attentiveness to duty was amazing and inspiring. Food supplies for the horses continued critical. The ground produced nothing in many places and only whitish grass in others. Villars was forced to divide his cavalry into small units so that the horses might have grass and to keep the infantrymen from butchering them for food. All of these difficulties, which were aggravated over a period of many months, forced Villars to write Louis XIV that he must soon seek a decision by combat or face the inevitable dissolution of the army. By trusting to God and the ability of the French soldier to defend himself, they might draw or even win a battle. Louis XIV wrote that he had confidence in him but that France could not risk any general action.[20]

Tournai continued to resist the best allied efforts. On July 28, during a violent rainstorm, Villars penetrated with four hundred grenadiers to within five miles of the city and held a conference with Sûrville's representative, who reported that Sûrville was still resisting from the citadel. Believing that his right flank would be in danger if Tournai fell, Villars shifted his center to a position between Douai and Denain where he concentrated forty-five battalions, leaving only six entrenched in a series of strong points along the Scarpe. It was well that he had done so, because on the evening of August 8 the Duke of Marlborough attempted a surprise attack on Marchiennes. Seizing his op-

19 Villars, Luxembourg to Voisin, July 7-9, AG 2151.
20 AG 2151, 117, 175, 177, 185, 205, 219, 221, 232, 262, 295, AG 2152, 8, 12, 80; Maintenon to Villars, n.d., in De Vogüé, *Correspondance*, I, 330ff.

portunity, Villars opened fire and prepared for a general resistance, but Marlborough retired without returning the fire. For the remainder of August Villars dug ever deeper, and when on September 3 the citadel of Tournai ran up the white flag, the Army of Flanders was prepared for the loss.[21]

Now that the combined army of Eugene and Marlborough was released for field action, Villars expected an attack. He did not intend to offer passive resistance to be followed by a retreat, planning instead to put up a fight while maneuvering between his interior entrenchments. Since a battle seemed inevitable, another request had long since gone out for a prince of the blood. Again the Bourbons remained at court. Failing with the king, Villars wrote Madame de Maintenon asking for her intercession. She replied that Louis would not let the princes leave his side, though continuing to place his faith in God and Villars.[22]

Although there was no thought of relieving him, it did occur to the minions at court that, if Villars offered himself to the enemy fire as was his habit, he might be killed without another marshal in Flanders to take his place. The only available person of sufficient rank was the ancient Boufflers. Ordered to Flanders, the old marshal refused to go unless he could serve under Villars—an answer that must have rocked Versailles. Louis XIV agreed, and the initial meeting of the two marshals was very cordial, each demanding that the other take command. However, Villars fully intended to hold the reins of command or resign. The military record of Boufflers—especially his able defense of Lille in 1708— gave the Army of Flanders a needed boost in morale.[23]

Villars could do little but wait for Prince Eugene and the

21 AG 2151, 212-30, AG 2152, 2-207; Marlborough to Walpole, July 11, to Boyle, August 8, 12, in Murray, *Correspondence*, IV, 542, 569ff, 572; Rechberger, *Feldzug 1709*, 210, 215, 219, 228ff, 253, 271.

22 Villars to Maintenon, July 29, in De Vogüé, *Correspondance*, I, 324ff; Maintenon to Villars, August 2, in De Vogüé, *Maintenon et Villars*, 51ff; Villars to Voisin, September 1, AG 2152.

23 Boufflers to Villars, September 3, AG 2152; Villars to Voisin, September 2, AG 2152.

Duke of Marlborough. On September 4, after sending several detachments to make covering demonstrations at La Basse, the major portion of the allied force, which had been camped around Orchies, crossed the Escault at Mortagne and took the road for Mons. Their design seemed to be another siege. Villars decided to entrench himself in their path. But the flying detachments he ordered out arrived on the Laine one hour after the allied advance guard had secured a bridgehead. On learning of this, he gave the necessary orders for a concentration at Hognenau.[24]

Couriers raced from unit to unit collecting every available gun, horse, man, and dram of powder for what all expected to be the deciding battle of the war. The court held its breath as the tension settled over the coming field of battle. On the evening of September 7 the hastily reinforced French army was camped facing northeast between Athis and Montreuil while the allies were established with Eugene to the west of Mons and Marlborough to the south around Quiry. Villars wished to seek a separate action with Marlborough but unfortunately had to wait for a bread convoy. Eugene marched for Marlborough's camp that same day.[25]

Only a range of very dense woods separated the opposing armies. The largest passage through the woods was that centering on the small town of Malplaquet. The small valley was only one mile wide lying between the woods of Sars and Lanière. On the night of September 8 Villars posted large detachments of cavalry at the head of the woods while the infantry began to entrench in the woods in the following manner: After clearing a space about fifty paces

24 Villars, Boufflers, Louis XIV, September 4, 6, AG 2152; Eugene to the Emperor, September 4, in Rechberger, *Feldzug 1709*, 275.
25 For the events centering on the battle of Malplaquet, see Villars to Louis XIV, September 10, AG 2152; Boufflers to Louis XIV, September 11, BN 2062; official French account, AG 2152, 206; Marlborough to Queen Anne and Boyle, September 11, in Murray, *Correspondence*, IV, 591ff; account of Frezilière, AG A4, VII, #3, 85; Count of Lagnac to Elector of Saxony, AG, *Mémoires historiques*, VIII, 72, 86-88; Marlborough's and Eugene's dispositions, AG, *Mémoires historiques*, VIII, 12, 24, 76, 85.

wide every five hundred paces, the French set up a fortified barrier on their side of the clearing. On both sides of the woods strong interlocking entrenchments were constructed.

At dawn on September 9, masked by their positions and troops already in the woods, the French army paraded in order of battle before Malplaquet. The enemy was not aware of the French moves until nearly 8 A.M. To determine the intentions of the French, Marlborough sent forward thirty squadrons and 400 grenadiers with orders to retire when the French made threatening noises. In the Anglo-Dutch camp there was great confusion, as most of the horses had been sent to forage and many of the men were at breakfast.

Villars would never again have such an opportunity. With just over two miles separating the allied armies, he might have fallen on the Anglo-Dutch and put them to rout before Eugene could march onto the field. There has been a lively discussion as to why Villars, who was usually so impetuous, failed to attack. But when the battlefield and other circumstances are carefully analyzed, the reader will realize that Villars was facing two armies, either of which outnumbered his entire force. This was the last-ditch stand of France, and that knowledge must have weighed heavily on Villars. Lastly, the French army was concentrated in a strong defensive position.

The tattered French line stood to arms for most of the day and camped in ranks for the night. The soldiers worked in shifts throughout the night putting the finishing touches on the fortifications. At dawn on the tenth a cannonade began that lasted all day without visible effect on either side. The Duke of Marlborough and Prince Eugene spent the day beating back the arguments of the Dutch deputies as to why they should not attack. Finally a plan was drawn up. A simultaneous attack would be launched on both flanks of the French army—thirty battalions against the French left, under the Prince of Orange, and eighty-two battalions on the left, under Eugene, with the objective of breaking the French right flank. Marlborough held thirty-three English battalions in reserve with the understanding that, if the French weakened their center position to reinforce one or both flanks, he would assault the redoubts. All the allied cavalry was massed in column in reserve. The allied artillery was formed into several large parks to rake the French center. On his side Villars had twenty battalions on the left, thirteen in the center, thirty-six on the right, and seventy in reserve under his personal command. The French artillery was distributed up and down the line, and the cavalry was in reserve on the extreme flanks.

At dawn on September 11 a thick fog covered the field and forced the allies to hold their attack. Villars took this opportunity to canter with his entire staff out in front of his forward lines. As word of this supposed bravado spread through the French army, there were repeated cheers of "Vive le maréchal." The French line obviously did not realize that Villars could not be seen by the allies. While Villars pranced up and down, the allies were holding divine services. At about 7:30 A.M. the sun dissipated the fog making a beautiful day in autumn—an illusion quickly destroyed as the French gunners opened fire on the tightly packed allied formations with telling effect. The allies returned the fire, but French infantry losses were very light as their line stood behind field fortifications. However, the French cavalry suffered heavily. It was just after eight o'clock when the imperial battalions, animated by the presence of Prince Eugene, began to assault the French left flank. Closer and closer the imperial lines came to the French entrenchments. At approximately fifty paces the allies met with their first surprise of the day. The Brigades of Brittany and Provence began firing volleys from their trenches. At almost point-blank range the method of firing by alternation of a four-line formation had a most deadly effect on the leading imperial battalions, which seemed to dissolve like butter in the hot sun. But thanks to numerical superiority and at the price of heavy bloodshed, the imperials slowly forced the French line back.

At this point the allies received their second shock of the day. The French infantry battalions, which were so poor looking and obviously undermanned, retired step by step in a four-line formation, turning with parade-ground precision to deliver volleys at the voice commands of a rapidly diminishing number of officers. Time and time again the gradually shrinking French line closed up on command and presented their bayonets to the enemy lines.

Seeing the difficulty of the left flank, Villars sent first the Brigade of Champagne and then the Irish Regiment to bolster the ever lessening fire of his troops. With these reinforcements the left flank was gradually able to disengage itself from the overly close quarters with the imperials. Villars now took the mass of fifty battalions remaining to him and began, at the quickstep with the lusty cheers of the French line ringing in his ears, to lead personally on horseback a counterattack. As the French line came within range the imperials volleyed, shooting the horse out from under Villars and killing most of his staff. When Villars tried to remount, a ball from the second volley struck him in the knee. His life was spared only because Lieutenant Generals Chémérault and Albergotti threw themselves in front of him as the imperials volleyed yet a third time.

The French infantry reserve ground to a halt. Despite the frantic pleadings and orders from the irate Villars, he was carried from the field by his personal grenadier company, which did not stop until he was safe behind the guns of Quesnoy. Unfortunately the first lines of the French battalions had seen the marshal carried from the field. Word resounded from unit to unit that Villars was dead. Since the entire general staff had been killed or wounded, the French left flank, that now contained the entire infantry reserve, was thrown into a state of confusion. But it did not break and run.

On the French right flank the Dutch infantry, led by the Prince of Orange, began its attack one-half hour later. The Dutch stormed into the French positions in the woods of Lanière. Taken in enfilade and front simultaneously, the Prince of Orange lost his horse, and the two leading battalions were reduced from 1,500 each to forty-nine and forty-seven respectively. But with their usual tenacity the Dutch kept up their assault and pierced the outer French works at two points, planting their ensigns on the palisades. But dodging behind trees for five hundred paces, the now ragged Dutch line ran into the Brigade of Navarre behind palisades. Navarre fired and then charged at bayonet point. The confused, muddled fight in the woods was murderous for both sides, but the exhausted Dutch gradually gave ground until the French again controlled their forward fortifications.

Seeing what appeared to be an enemy rout developing, the Marshal Boufflers, as yet unaware of Villars' misfortune and the confusion on the French left flank, ordered the right flank to remain in place until he communicated with the commander-in-chief. Across the field of battle, after having the attack on the French left stalled and the charge on the right repulsed, Marlborough advanced with the English battalions on the French center. Once his infantry controlled the center, he planned to put his cavalry through the breach.

Boufflers, who had finally learned of Villars' personal disaster and of the precarious position of the French reserve, ordered the French and Swiss guards in the center entrenchments to hold their ground until he could move units from the left flank to support them. But even before his messenger could reach the left of the French line, the guards fled after firing one volley, leaving the English in complete control of the center. Through this breach fifty squadrons charged. Boufflers galloped over to the reserve cavalry units stationed on his flank. On the clear note of the charge the *Maison du Roi, gendarmes, chevaux-légers,* and musketeers advanced at the walk, then the trot, and finally the gallop, as Boufflers' flashing saber waved in the sun. But the instant before contact the well-trained enemy cavalry retired behind the British grenadiers, and the French mounts ran into a blazing wall of fire.

Now the French cavalry and dragoon regiments, under the command of Major Generals De Magnac and Coigny, began to advance. Old Boufflers, as if in his second youth, galloped up with his bugler and led them. Again the story was the same, as the stout English infantry held the French horsemen. The allies had now brought up the bulk of their cavalry, and six times their lines charged and then separated to charge again. At 3:30 P.M. the exhausted Boufflers learned that his left flank was being turned by General Withers' brigade advancing from Sars through the woods. Aware that the outnumbered French units were beginning to reel, Boufflers ordered a general retreat.

On the left, the French line retired in excellent order with drums beating and flags flying while the Knight of Rozel held the rear-guard position, beating off the very weak allied attempts at pursuit. In the center, Major General Saint-Hilaire very calmly backed up the horses and pulled off the French cannon and ammunition. The right flank was thrown into some confusion when the Brigade of Navarre had to be ordered from the field three times. Finally a personal plea from the badly wounded Lieutenant General Artagnan persuaded them to retreat. Surprisingly the Army of Flanders lost only about 500 prisoners, mostly stragglers and wounded.

The only reasonable explanation of why Marlborough (Eugene had been hospitalized by a slight head wound) did not pursue the French was that the allies were so grievously hurt that they were incapable of immediately reforming. The allied casualties had been so large that Marlborough requested and received a three-day truce in order to clear the battlefield of the dead and wounded. Casualty figures for such a confused, tangled engagement are extremely difficult to establish. However, after a careful perusal of the source material, the most reliable figures seem to be: for the Army of Eugene and Marlborough, 24,263 killed and wounded; for the Army of Flanders, between 10,000 and 12,000 killed and wounded.[26]

While it is true that Malplaquet must strictly count as an allied victory since they held the field of battle at the end of the day, the forward advance of Eugene and Marlborough had indeed been checked. Also, as future events proved, the allies never again allowed Villars to choose the field of battle. Possibly the fanatical quality demonstrated by the French soldiers gave the allied commanders some concern. For in eighteenth-century Europe, the concept of fighting to the last man was almost unknown except in the tactics of one individual, Claude Louis Hector de Villars.

From his stretcher Villars dashed off a letter to the king in which he asked for permission to fight again so that the enemy army might be completely destroyed. Louis XIV was not of a mind to permit any further such actions. Naturally the allied army, freed from fear of attack, proceeded to invest Mons.[27]

While Villars' career with the army was ended for the year,

26 Boufflers to Voisin, September 14, AG 2152. The printed sources available failed to shed any additional light upon this subject. Stanhope quotes a letter to Godolphin in which Marlborough states that he had "proposed a suspension of arms for two days during which time the dead might be buried and the wounded be relieved" (Philip Stanhope, *History of England* . . . [London, 1870], II, 122). The figure for the allied loss comes from AG *Mémoires historiques*, VIII, 72, in which the French general staff in the early twentieth century checked the archives of all the states having contingents in the allied army. Only an estimation can be given of the French losses simply because no set of official statistics exists.

27 Villars, Louis XIV, Boufflers, Voisin, September 11-13, 15, AG 2152.

he was still to be the center of attention. The surgeons began to fear that his wound would prove fatal. Since the kneecap was cracked with the ball lodged behind the cap, they spoke of amputation. On learning of their intention, Villars ordered his faithful grenadiers to shoot anyone who attempted such an operation. But a fever did set in, and the flesh around the wound began to rot. Finding that his strength was dwindling, Villars called for extreme unction and appeared to be tranquilly waiting for death. Madame Villars had arrived in camp to nurse her husband. She wrote Madame de Maintenon that, unless something was quickly done, the marshal would die. The king made Villars a peer of France. But stopped from amputation by the marshal's watchful servants, the four attending surgeons had Boufflers request the attendance of Marchand, first surgeon to the king. This skilled man arrived in three days, looked at the knee, probed for the ball, and cauterized the wound. The fever fell and Villars began to eat. But there was every reason to doubt that he would ever regain the use of his knee.[28]

In the field the French defenders of Mons were yielding one bastion at a time as the city was gradually and grimly reduced. Saint-Simon expressed the position of the army best when he wrote that it was again grave. No bread, no money, no replacements, and little ammunition again characterized the Army of Flanders. In such a position Boufflers could do nothing except beg for supplies and weep when Mons capitulated on October 20.[29]

Despite his demands, Villars was confined to bed by royal order. Forty-three days after Malplaquet, Le Dran and Duraudin, his attending surgeons, tried to remove some rotting flesh. After tying Villars fast to a table and using

28 Louis XIV, Boufflers, Voisin, September 20, 26, 30, October 2, 4, 5, AG 2152, 2153: Madame de Villars to Maintenon, September 2, in Maintenon, *Lettres*, VII, 279ff.
29 Saint-Simon, *Mémoires*, XVI, 383ff.

four large men further to immobilize him, they cut away. Despite the terrible pain, he remained conscious—and despite the vast quantity of brandy he had consumed. Madame de Villars was informed that the infection had been arrested.[30]

For his return to Paris, Villars left Quesnoy with an imposing equipage. His bed was fitted into a royal carriage. A platoon of cavalry galloped ahead while the grenadiers attending his person rode in gaily bedecked wagons. All along the route the marshal was met with cheers. At the Château of Harnicourt the physician again closed the wound. Villars was far from recovered. At the end of the sixth day the entourage arrived in Paris where he was installed in his bedchamber on the Rue de Grenelle. In less than a week Louis XIV ordered him moved to Versailles and placed in the apartment of the Prince of Conti, who left for an extended vacation on his country estates. As soon as the marshal was safely in his bed, Louis XIV rushed into the room and embraced him. To mark further his favor the king returned that same afternoon. Saint-Simon, who, because of his high rank, was present at both of these meetings, said that it had been thirty years since the king had shown such attention to one of his servants. The court hurriedly fell into line. The Dauphin, the Duke and Duchess of Bourgogne, the secretaries of state, and Madame de Maintenon led the parade. As the year 1709 closed, Villars had indeed arrived at the highest pinnacle of recognition possible in the reign of Louis XIV for the son of a *petit frondeur*.[31]

30 Boufflers to Voisin, October 7, AG 2153; Voisin to Boufflers, October 14, BN 20625; Madame de Villars to Boufflers, n.d., AG 2153, 27.
31 Dangeau, *Journal*, XIII, 55-78; Saint-Simon, *Mémoires*, XVI, 219, 303ff, 307.

CHAPTER SEVEN

Defender of the Realm, 1710-1711

JUST AS THE OPPORTUNITIES FOR A BRILLIANT AND DECISIVE campaign were opening to the allies, their ability to take advantage of them was diminishing. In England the strain of the long war was making itself felt in spite of the accessions to her colonies and her supremacy over the sea. The year of Malplaquet saw the Duchess of Marlborough dismissed from her court appointments. Every European government knew that the ascendancy of the Duchess of Marlborough over the mind of Queen Anne was a thing of the past. In this state of affairs Marlborough did not dare to run the risk of a doubtful offensive campaign. He now planned methodically to drive Villars back from one position to another—that is to reduce France by one fortress at a time.

In the spring of 1710 Prince Eugene and the Duke of Marlborough concentrated a powerful army of 171 full-strength battalions around Tournai. On April 20 the allied army merely probed the French entrenchments near Cambrai. Much to the amazement of Marlborough and Eugene, the French infantry turned and ran without even a token resistance. The allies invested Douai. The 156 battalions of the Army of Flanders were down to an average of 250 men, many of whom lacked even serviceable weapons. The morale of the French army had reached its lowest point. Villars wrote from his sickbed that the news from Flanders was disheartening. The lack of hope on his part marked a new low in the fortunes of France during the War of the Spanish Succession. Perhaps his physical condition was partly to blame for such a gloomy outlook. He was still suffering intensely from his wound. The royal surgeons had devised an iron apparatus to give the knee support. But Villars wrote that pain was his constant companion. He could not stand without the support of a heavy cane. But Marshal Villars was once again, in the spring of 1710, the last resource of the House of Bourbon.[1]

Villars was carried to the theater of operations in a sedan chair. On May 12 the Army of Flanders began to concentrate on Cambrai. Determined to defend his king, Villars painfully mounted a horse for a reconnaissance and to attempt to revive the drooping spirits of the French line by his presence and that of his flag. Unfortunately he relied too much on his weak physical powers. Marshal Montesquiou wrote to Voisin that Villars refused to be paraded in a sedan chair. The marshal had mounted a horse only to be thrown into a ditch. But determination prevailed and, despite all the protests and dire warnings of his physicians, he ordered himself strapped to his horse. In this manner he could sit erect for several hours without losing consciousness.[2]

Despite the lack of equipment, men, and morale and his

[1] Dangeau, *Journal*, XIII, 81, 93ff, 142, 146, 153; Villars' lack of hope, AG 2213, 196, AG 2214, 30. Carl Freiherrn von Hipssich, *Spanischer Succes-sions-Krieg, Feldzug 1710* (Vienna: 1887), 587-90, gives the orders of battle for the allied armies. A similar order of battle for the Army of Flanders lists 153 battalions and 258 squadrons, but AG 2214, 86-107, gives strength reports for the various French units; Marlborough to Boyle, April 20, 23, in Murray, *Correspondence*, IV, 721ff, V, 3ff; Eugene to the Emperor, April 30, May 4, in Hipssich, *Feldzug 1710*, 57, 64; De Vogüé, *Mémoires*, III, 80ff.

[2] Montesquiou to Voisin, May 18, AG 2215; Dangeau, *Journal*, XIII, 153, 156ff; Eugene to the Emperer, May 11, 18, in Hipssich, *Feldzug 1710*, 74, 84; Marlborough to Boyle, May 12, in Murray *Correspondence*, V, 21ff; De Vogüé, *Mémoires*, III, 81ff.

own physical distress, Villars began to march to the relief of
Douai on May 25. On the eighth day the Army of Flanders
came into view of the allied lines, which stretched from
the right at Harne to Vitry on the Scarpe. The allies met
the French with silence from behind a strong series of
fortifications. To attack such a position with a far numer-
ically and spiritually inferior force was more than Villars
would have tried in his more audacious prime, let alone now,
when his quick mind was dulled by constant pain. With a
spark of his former self he lashed out at the redoubt of
Brache, driving the small garrison from its position. The
cautious Marlborough simply flooded the area before his
left flank. There were to be no more Malplaquets. If
Villars wanted to fight he would have to do so on the ground
and under the conditions chosen by the allies. Louis XIV
had said, "Risk nothing. Stall, delay—while I negotiate."
In 1710 the enfeebled Villars was the willing servant of his
royal master.[3]

In complete compliance with his instructions to remain
on the defensive, Villars entrenched behind the Scarpe with
his right at Oisy and his left behind Mouchy. A strong
corps was stationed between Bouchain and Valenciennes.
Hardly had these entrenchments been completed when
Douai capitulated on June 26. All Villars could do was to
reinforce the garrisons of Béthune and Aire and wait for
developments. The allies, always covered by the Scarpe,
extended their right to Saint-Pol and their left to the Abbey
of Saint-Eloi. Following the movements of the enemy,
Villars shifted his right toward Arras and his left south
of Aubigny.[4]

These tactics, so necessary in a campaign of position, were

3 For the deficiencies of supplies and manpower, see May 16-24, AG 2215;
Villars to Voisin, May 26, AG 2215; Marlborough to Boyle, May 26, 27, in
Murray, Correspondence, V, 33ff; Eugene to the Emperor, June 1, in
Hipssich, Feldzug 1710, 107; Villars to Louis XIV, June 3, AG 2215.
4 See June 5-26, AG 2215; Hipssich, Feldzug 1710, June 11, 15-20; Marl-
borough to Boyle, June 19, in Murray, Correspondence, V, 53ff.

not in keeping with the principles or the spirit of the marshal. Villars began to beg for permission to attack even while admitting that, although the Army of Flanders looked very large on paper, the second line of the infantry did not exist and that the cavalry squadrons were only one-third their normal strength. If the food had somewhat improved since 1709, the soldiers were still discontented from the lack of everything else. The officers had not been paid in almost eighteen months. Despite his efforts to shoot all of them, the usurers were still in operation and were discounting the paper money by 80 percent. To add to Villars' troubles, his knee had become infected again. It was reported that he had been carried unconscious to one side more than once only to revive and to remount to give the soldiers courage. Villars wrote Voisin that the "damnable iron contraption" had not permitted him to gallop and, if he could not gallop, how could he fight? Apparently Villars threw the false knee away. The pain must have been intense.[5]

The allies had repaired, provisioned, and garrisoned Douai. They now marched on Béthune. The French cavalry was dashed to pieces in futile attempts to delay the investiture of the fortress, which by July 16 was surrounded and under siege. Once again the allied army of observation dug in between Aubigny and Saint-Pol with the left resting on the Scarpe and the right on the small stream Ternoise. Rightly judging it impossible to attack, Villars moved his left to Hesdin, placed his right on the Scarpe and covered his center by a long series of entrenchments. Despite frantic letters from Villars, Louis XIV would not give him any freedom of action and absolutely prohibited any thought of a combat. But when on August 30 a strong enemy detachment tested the strength of the French entrenchments, Villars braced himself for an attack. The probe turned out

5 Villars to Louis XIV, Voisin, AG 2215, 64, 134, 163, 177, 196, 207, 218, AG 2216, 33; Villars to Maintenon, June 12, in De Vogüé, *Maintenon et Villars*, 55.

to be a feint, and when two days later Villars heard of the fall of Béthune the entire allied army was on its way north in the direction of Lille.[6]

Determined to harass the allied route of march, Villars left his camp at the head of forty squadrons with the full intention of attacking the allied rear guard. But Marlborough had taken precautions. Villars found that he could not attack without risking a general battle, a thing which he was forbidden to do. On his further and more violent pleadings, Louis XIV informed Villars that he would be replaced immediately by Marshal Harcourt. Thus, when the allies came to invest Aire-sur-Lys, they were successful because of Marlborough's feint plus the refusal of Louis XIV to allow Villars any freedom of action. With the opening of this third siege it became apparent to all that Marlborough did not want another pitched battle but had determined to conquer France fortress by fortress. To give his English opponent something to remember him by, Villars sent twelve battalions and six regiments of dragoons to attack a heavily laden supply convoy of fifty large barges escorted by 2,000 cavalry. The ambush was a complete success. The barges were burned and the escort entirely killed or captured.[7]

Villars left the army as soon as Harcourt arrived on September 25 and went to Bourbonne for the baths, seeking a final cure for the troublesome knee. He wrote Voisin that he had only about one-sixth of the normal movement in the knee and that the water really was doing very little good. Furthermore he was in pain all the time. To show that he bore the marshal no ill will, Louis XIV gave Villars the governorship of Metz, perhaps also hinting that the Flanders theater was overly taxing. But when Villars returned to

6 See June 26-31, AG 2215, July 1-August 30, AG 2216, September 1, AG 2217; Eugene to the Emperor, July 2, in Hipssich, *Feldzug 1710*, 198; Murray, *Correspondence*, V, July 7, 10, 14, 17, August 30, September 1.
7 Villars, Voisin, Louis XIV, Ravignac, September 2-21, AG 2217.

Paris his knee, more improved perhaps from inactivity than the curative powers of the waters, supported his weight. On the same day (November 8) that Villars walked unaided into his sovereign's presence Aire capitulated to the allies.[8]

The campaigning season of 1710 ended with France shorn of a few more fortresses and in a critical position along the northern frontier. Villars, hampered by ill health, an outnumbered, dispirited army, and royal interference, had been able to accomplish nothing. The actions of the allies in refusing to fight leaves no doubt that they did not want another bloodbath. As for Louis XIV, he could not run the risk, as another Malplaquet would completely ruin his army and more than likely snuff out the life of his most competent marshal, who would not stay behind the lines. The strategy of the Sun King was to wear the allies down, to break the alliance by diplomacy, and to sicken them of war by the numerous casualties that a besieger always suffers in comparison to a defending force.

The material or tactical situation did not improve over the winter months. But when in April 1711 Villars returned to general headquarters, now at Arras, he went with an approved plan to retake Douai. The Duke of Marlborough had concocted a similar plan to attack Arras. While the French were stealthily advancing toward Arleux behind the Sensée, the allies were just as quietly marching toward them on the opposite bank in the direction of Arras. The mutual consternation must have been enormous when both armies reached the same crossing on the Sensée at the same time. As neither was prepared for battle, the two armies, after several sharp but ragged exchanges, by tacit consent, stacked arms and began to fraternize. Small gifts were exchanged by the common soldiers. Villars rode over to the allied head-

[8] Dangeau, *Journal*, XIII, 197ff, 272ff; Villars to Voisin, September 25, October 8, AG 2217; Marlborough to Boyle, September 29, in Murray, *Correspondence*, V, 167; De Vogüé, *Mémoires*, III, 102.

quarters taking James III along for a lark. The presence of the pretender threw the English staff into confusion, but the smiling Marlborough soon restored order. After a lively and long entertainment, Villars and James III rode back across the river. A letter from Marlborough soon arrived advising a little more prudence in the future and more caution on the part of James on his promenades because someone might decide to shoot him.[9]

After this brief tête-à-tête both sides turned to more practical considerations. It was soon apparent that the allies would not attack and that Villars was forbidden to assume the offensive. Embarrassment must have been general when for fifteen days the two armies sat facing each other, neither wanting to be the first to retire. On May 13 Marlborough sounded the call to arms in his camp. The French formed into line of battle. Although the two armies paraded to within three hundred paces of each other, no shot was fired. Marlborough, seeing that he could not panic the master intimidator, returned to camp for further consultations.[10]

Villars during this time did not neglect to initiate a series of harassing operations which soon proved a major headache for the allied supply convoys, isolated units, and the allied baggage trains, which found themselves being cut to pieces by the French cavalry, which appeared never to sleep. He demanded reinforcements, but Louis XIV replied by detaching twenty battalions and thirty squadrons for duty on the Rhine. However, it was some relief that the material situation of the army improved daily. At least there was now a constant supply of bread and meat, weapons that would fire, boots, and powder that would burn. Villars proudly reported that he had not had to punish a single

9 Villars, Voisin, Montesquiou, Louis XIV, April 7-26, AG 2303; Friedrich Freiherrn Mühliverth-Gartner, *Spanischer Successions-Krieg, Feldzug 1711* (Vienna, 1887), 469ff, 143-48.

10 Villars to Voisin, May 5, 9, 11, 13, AG 2303; De Vogüé, *Mémoires*, III, 107.

man in forty-three days and that discipline was superb in the face of a far superior enemy. He said in a letter to Voisin that the army was indeed small but the soldiers now considered the enemy afraid and could not understand why they could not attack.[11]

On June 14 the allies suddenly marched, establishing their right at Lens and their left towards Douai. The French army followed along, camping with its right at the Abbey of Etrun, its center at Arras and its left at the Château of Arleux. With his front covered by the Scarpe, Villars spanned the river in a dozen places to give the impression that his army might rush across at any moment. From this easily defensible position he sent a courier to Louis XIV demanding permission to attack north of the river. He reasoned that a war of siege was a safe course but that France would soon be out of fortresses and that it was better to fight before the army was forced to retire deep into France. But the king replied that Villars was to maintain a defensive posture and under no circumstances to seek a battle. This royal decision was based on the fact that the French peace overtures to England were beginning to meet with some success.[12]

On June 27 Villars was ordered to send another ten battalions and twenty-six squadrons to Alsace where Marshal Harcourt was attempting to force the Duke of Württemburg from the war. But the enemy, who was informed of this movement, profited by surprising Arleux. Villars personally led thirty squadrons in an unsuccessful attempt to

[11] Villars to Louis XIV, May 10, AG 2303; Marlborough to St. John, May 11, 14, in Murray, *Correspondence,* V, 336, 342ff; Villars to Voisin, May 13, 16, June 2, 9, AG 2303, 2304; Voisin to Villars, May 22, 27, AG 2303, June 3, AG 2304; Eugene to Charles III of Spain, June 7, in Mühliverth-Gartner, *Feldzug 1711,* 32.

[12] Villars, Montesquiou, Louis XIV, June 13-19, AG 2304; Eugene to the Empress, June 16, in Mühliverth-Gartner, *Feldzug 1711,* 42; Villars to Maintenon, June 19, 23, in De Vogüé, *Correspondance,* I, 389ff; Marlborough to Eugene, June 21, in Murray, *Correspondence,* V, 382; Villars to Voisin, June 20, 22, 26, AG 2304.

retake the position. The marshal was not one to let such an affront go unpunished. On July 10 he decided to attack an isolated enemy post between Douai and Gueulzin. In a brilliant cavalry action, thirty squadrons of dragoons surprised the imperials. The enemy camp was destroyed and some 1,200 survivors were captured.[13]

The loss of the small place of Arleux began to constitute a real menace to Villars' right flank, as the allies continued to reinforce their garrison there. On July 22 Villars sent Marshal Montesquiou, his second in command, to attack Arleux. In obvious imitation of his superior and friend, Montesquiou dismounted and, saber in hand, led the French infantry up to, over, and through the enemy garrison. Villars held up Montesquiou's conduct as the type expected of all officers. This success was more than counterbalanced by a serious check. While French attention was on the Scarpe, Marlborough descended on Bouchain on the night of August 14, seizing the fortress by a *coup de main* almost before the startled garrison could answer the call to arms. This was the first real advantage gained by the allies in an entire campaigning season. Important because of the revived allied morale, the fall of Bouchain further depressed the spirits of the French. But the two armies continued to face each other for the remainder of the campaigning season without seeking a decision. Powerful diplomatic forces now at work could not permit even the possibility of a defeat for either side.[14]

The campaigns of 1710 and 1711 were technically successful for the allies. Only by the most arduous efforts had the French kept their enemies from penetrating the heart of France, but keep them out they did! However, little by little,

13 Villars, Voisin, Contades, June 27-July 6, AG 2304; Marlborough to St. John, June 29, July 2, in Murray, *Correspondence*, V, 399ff; Eugene to the Empress, July 7, in Mühliverth-Gartner, *Feldzug 1711*, 47.
14 Villars, Montesquiou, July 19-August 14, AG 2304, 2305; Eugene to Charles III, July 31, in Mühliverth-Gartner, *Feldzug 1711*, 50.

bit by bit, Vauban's defensive chain was falling. Lille, Douai, Béthune, Aire, and Bouchain were now in allied hands. It seemed, as Villars had once said, that the kingdom of France would soon have only the bayonets of her soldiers for protection.

The Rhine and the Italian fronts saw little of consequence in 1710-1711. Beyond sporadic border clashes, these theaters of war remained almost tranquil. After the withdrawal of all French troops from Spain in the summer of 1709, the allied army commanded by Stanhope and Stahremberg had first driven Philip V out of Aragon, occupied Madrid, and by the spring of 1710 was besieging Valladolid. The result of this series of allied successes was a national uprising of the Castilian Spaniards in favor of Philip V. In June 1710 Louis sent Marshal Vendôme to command the Spanish army. Far more threatened by the harassing actions of the Spanish guerillas than by Vendôme's maneuvers, Stanhope and Stahremberg abandoned Madrid, split their forces, and were defeated separately. By the end of 1711 the allies held only Barcelona. This success in Spain meant little, however, as long as the Marlborough-Eugene combination continued gradually to reduce the fortress system in northern France.

By very good fortune and, one might say, in the nick of time, Louis XIV's peace negotiations bore fruit. England seemed almost ready to leave the war. Marlborough's party in Parliament was tottering. The subsidy system by which England shouldered a large share of the cost of the Dutch and Habsburg armies had given England the unprecedented public debt of £ 50,684,956. The Tory party, which had regained power in the elections of 1710, would open a peace conference in the first month of 1712. The government in London had fought to prevent a Bourbon empire like that of Charles V. But, at the end of 1711, the war had already lasted ten years with France showing an uncanny ability to fight on despite military defeat and severe famine. The

Habsburg armies had stripped the Bourbon Philip V of his possessions in the Milanese and the Low Countries. The untimely death of Emperor Joseph I had once again united all the ancient Habsburg territorial claims in one pretender. It certainly would not be in the interests of England to have Charles VI, who as Charles III laid claim to the Spanish throne, reconstitute his namesake's empire. As for her own position, England was now the undisputed mistress of the seas. Her conquest of Gibraltar and occupation of Minorca gave her control of the western Mediterranean. For all these reasons the most powerful nation of the coalition decided to leave the war late in 1711 and to make a separate peace if necessary. Despite partial success in Spain and near inaction along the Rhine, the military position of France in the winter of 1711 was dismal, but there was hope on the diplomatic horizon.

CHAPTER EIGHT

The Puzzle That Was Denain, 1712

THE CONGRESS OF UTRECHT OPENED ON JANUARY 29, 1712. Representatives of the Dutch Empire, Habsburg, Portuguese, and Savoyards attended only out of fear that the Anglo-French negotiations might take England out of the war. The attitude of the new English government was made explicit in Marlborough's replacement by the Duke of Ormond. Emperor Charles VI did not wish a negotiated peace. He was determined to dictate peace to a humbled Bourbon. The general situation gave every indication that the Habsburg would succeed. Louis XIV could put only greatly inferior forces into the coming campaign against a powerful, well provisioned and numerous army under the overall command of Prince Eugene. Therefore the attitude of all save the English and French at Utrecht was to wage a vigorous campaign throughout the next season. Allied reasoning held that the loss of one more series of forts would open the road to Paris.

In the early spring of 1712 Eugene established the 100,000 man allied army between the Escaut and the Sambre. From this position the allies equally menaced Quesnoy and Landrecies. Should these two fortresses fall, there would be no

obstacle which could arrest their march on Paris. Powerful
imperial cavalry units penetrated Champagne, threatening
Rheims. Louis XIV did not have more than 70,000 men for
the Army of Flanders. Marshal Villars was again designated
to command in the north and ordered to court for a personal audience with the king. Villars went to Marly on
April 12 for the interview. The king had just suffered the
loss of his grandson, granddaughter, and great-grandson.
Moved by Villars' genuine expressions of sympathy, Louis
XIV cast aside his regal attitude for a moment saying, "You
know my personal problems. There are few examples in
history of a man who in the space of a few weeks has lost
his grandson, granddaughter, and great-grandson. God is
punishing me and I deserve it. But I must forget my personal
grief and see what can be done for my kingdom. The confidence that I have in you has been marked by the command
of my armies and the personal honors I have given you.
I know your zeal and the bravery of my soldiers. But if
fortune should turn against you, what do you think my
course should be?" To such an important and unexpected
question Villars stood dazed and silent. The king went on,
"While giving you a little time to collect your thoughts,
I will tell you mine. I have heard all the arguments of my
counselors—that I must retire to Blois and not remain in
Paris if you are beaten. I know also that your army will
not be so routed that it will not be able to reform behind
the Somme. I know that river. It is very difficult to cross.
I intend to come to Peronne or Saint-Quentin, to gather there
all my remaining troops and to make a last effort by which
you and I will save the state or perish together. I do not
intend to live to see the enemy in my capital!"[1]

Villars, who now again was in possession of all his facul-
ties, replied, "Knowing the love of Your Majesty for glory,
I wish to take the liberty to say that the most glorious path

[1] De Vogüé, *Mémoires*, III, 138ff.

is also the wisest path, and I know of nothing that would be grander for a great prince than what Your Majesty plans to do." After such an audience Villars realized the responsibility of his own position as never before. But true to his character, the marshal looked upon the gloomy future without fear and with determination to be remembered as a heroic figure. He had been greatly impressed by the personal bravery of the king and was determined that his own should be no less.[2]

In spite of the best efforts of Daniel Voisin, the Army of Flanders lacked all types of supplies with the fortunate exception of food. In an army of 70,000, powder rations had to be carefully measured, and many artillery pieces lacked shot. Despite the deficiency of materials, Villars concentrated his forces between Marquion and Cambrai on the left bank of the Escaut on May 26. Prince Eugene was established behind the Seille between Le Cateau and Lieu Saint-Aman, thus isolating Quesnoy. The allies were supplied by river barges. But as the French-held towns of Valenciennes and Condé barred the passage of the Seille, Eugene established his supply base at Marchiennes on the Scarpe.[3]

While a powerful siege corps began to invest Quesnoy, Eugene entrenched the sixty-seven battalions and 220 squadrons of his army of observation along the Escaillon, with the left stretching towards Thiant. Between Thiant and the Escaut, seven battalions occupied a series of fortified posts to assure communications with Denain. At Denain the field fortifications built by Villars in 1709 were held by Lord Albermarle's twenty battalions and twenty-three squadrons. Two continuous parallel trenches set half a mile apart ran from Denain to the supply base at Marchiennes. The area

2 Anquetil, *Villars*, II, 199.
3 AG 2374, 171, 202, 209, 251, 278, 286, 302, 314; AG 2375, 47, 62, 197, 216; AG 2376, frontispiece, 5, 42, 68, 87, 118; Eugene to the Emperor, May 4, 15, 18, 22, in Heinrich Siegler Edlen von Eberswald, *Spanischer Successions-Krieg, Feldzug 1712* (Vienna, 1887), 69, 72, 73, 74, see also 116-41.

between the parallel trenches was used as a wagon road which Eugene named the "road to Paris." A distance of thirty-eight miles separated Landrecies and Marchiennes.[4]

The obvious weakness of these long defensive lines was first noticed by Lefebvre d'Orval, a member of the Parlement of Flanders. On May 27 D'Orval wrote Voisin that these fortifications might be attacked with some profit for the king—possibly without risk; the supply route of the enemy might be interrupted, thus relieving Quesnoy without a major engagement. D'Orval also wrote Villars, who answered only that he would take the matter under advisement. On June 15 D'Orval wrote again of his plan and pointed to the weakest spot in the allied line. The magistrate deemed it possible to carry the camp at Denain with the garrisons of Valenciennes and Cambrai if the main army would stage a diversion along the Seille. The court saw the merits of the project, and Voisin wrote Villars that the king would like to have it tried out. The marshal replied that he was giving the plan serious consideration.[5]

But Louis XIV had ordered Villars to stand on the defensive pending the outcome of the negotiations with England. "The principal object of the Army of Flanders," Voisin wrote, "is to keep the enemy from taking Landrecies. If you should consider that an attack on Denain would relieve Landrecies, go ahead, but if you feel that the fortress might still fall or that you would be risking a general action, do not attack Denain." Villars was quite naturally perplexed. Voisin soon added to his confusion by writing that, "The present situation does not permit a general action, but if you decide to use a part of your army in an attack on Denain, His Majesty is agreeable. The decision is yours."[6]

4 Villars to Voisin, May 22, AG 2376; Eberswald, *Feldzug 1712*, 132-47.
5 D'Orval, Voisin, Villars, May 27, 28, 31, June 6, 8, 13, 15, AG 2376, 2356, 2377.
6 Voisin to Villars, June 18, July 1, AG 2378, 2379.

Villars, undoubtedly remembering the audience and realizing that the court wanted a written guarantee of success,
hesitated and put off a final decision. The confusion in the
marshal's mind must have been absolute as he resorted to a
council of war for the first time in his military career, at
Noyelles on July 3. The lack of any solid success in the
long war had blunted the appetites of the general officers
for battle. To a man they recommended prudence and
caution. In fact, the council of war wanted the Army of
Flanders to retire to a line centering on the Oise and the
woods of Bohain and there to fortify in order to defend
Paris. When, in his turn, Villars proposed the attack on
Denain and a subsequent offensive, the generals were aghast
and not one showed the faintest tinge of enthusiasm.[7]

The fall of Quesnoy on the same day as the council of
war made a final decision on the Denain question all the
more pressing. Voisin wrote reproachfully that all Villars'
letters were filled with anxiety, but perhaps the marshal
should consider the anxiety of all France. The allies seemed
to be threatening both Valenciennes and Landrecies. With
Quesnoy firmly in his grip Eugene rejoined his siege corps
to the main army along the Escaillon. The importance of
the fall of Quesnoy and reinforcements to the allied army
did not escape D'Orval's sharp eye. He informed Voisin that
unless the Army of Flanders moved on Denain immediately
the chance would be lost forever. D'Orval asked for a field
commission and permission to attack the entrenched camp
of Lord Albermarle with only the garrison of Valenciennes.
When D'Orval suggested that the Escaut be bridged and
crossed at night, he completed the general outlines of the
plan used by Marshal Villars at Denain.[8]

The plan for severing Eugene's supply line seemed to have

[7] Villars to Voisin, July 3, AG 2379.
[8] D'Orval, Voisin, July 3, 6, 12, AG 2379; Eugene to the Emperor and
Zinzendorf, July 5, 12, in Eberswald, *Feldzug 1712*, 116, 119.

a better chance of success when the English signed an armistice at Marly on June 25. The English national troops, under the command of the Duke of Ormond, soon marched away. But Eugene, warned in advance, had already assured the mercenaries, heretofore paid by England, of their wages and hence their loyalty. Thus, even without the English, Eugene still possessed 122 battalions and 273 squadrons. Louis XIV had not lost sight of D'Orval's plan for attacking Denain. With the news of the diplomatic success, Voisin wrote Villars that, while the king's first thought in case Landrecies was besieged would be to interrupt the flow of supplies from Marchiennes, he had not personally reconnoitered the terrain and hence would rely on the marshal's judgment.[9]

Villars did seem to have abandoned the plan. It was almost as if the marshal were hypnotized by the danger to Landrecies and the fear of a final defeat. On July 17 Eugene sent thirty-four battalions and thirty-four squadrons to besiege Landrecies, and on the same day Louis XIV ordered Villars to march on the enemy and to fight, if necessary, to save Landrecies. In a new council of war on July 18 Villars laid out a plan. The Army of Flanders could cross the Escaut, march toward the sources of the Seille and move along the Sambre by Catillon, where they would reconnoiter the best way of relieving Landrecies. On the next day the French army moved all along the line and on the twentieth camped on the Upper Seille, with Villars' headquarters at Cateau-Cambrésis. In response, Prince Eugene removed many units from his right and approached Landrecies with the bulk of his army.[10]

Under the existing tactical situation, Villars judged an attack on Denain possible. On July 21 he decided to send

9 Eugene to the Emperor, Imperial War Council, order of battle, June 25, 26, in Eberswald, *Feldzug 1712*, 102, 104, 110, 400; Duke of Ormond, June 25, AG 2378; Voisin to Villars, July 6, AG 2422.

10 Eugene to the Emperor, July 17, in Eberswald, *Feldzug 1712*, 131; Louis XIV, Villars, July 12, 18, 20, AG 2380.

thirty battalions under the order of Lieutenants General de Broglie and Vieux-Pont. At the same time orders went out to the governor of Valenciennes to assist in the operation. Objections came from De Broglie and Vieux-Pont, who deemed the operation impossible without the participation of the entire army. Villars did not insist and wrote Voisin that he could find no one willing to lead an attack on Denain and that he was about to march for the Sambre.[11]

On July 22 the Army of Flanders was established facing Landrecies—its right flank on the Sambre near Mazingheim, its left towards Cateau—in full view of the allied army of observation. French dragoons could be seen searching out the shallow crossings along the river bank. That same evening, Villars led a small party across the Sambre on a personal reconnaissance. By dawn on July 23 he was within fusil range of the besiegers. He returned to the French lines disheartened, as he had learned that Eugene was indeed prepared.[12]

On the same day Villars made a decision that was to change the course of the war. He decided to countermarch, cross the Escaut and fall on Lord Albermarle's position with the entire Army of Flanders. Again the governor of Valenciennes was ordered to march for a junction with his garrison. The enterprise was accompanied with risk. If a single enemy soldier should spot the countermarch and report, all would be lost. Villars' plan was indeed audacious. He proposed to divide his army into four separate columns, countermarch twenty miles in the dark of night, converge five separate columns (the fifth was the garrison of Valenciennes) at one exact spot before dawn, cross a river, and overwhelm a heavily fortified place so quickly that Prince Eugene would not have time to intervene. The first condition of success was absolute secrecy. Villars confided only

11 Villars, De Broglie, July 21, AG 2380; Eugene to Albermarle, July 21, in Eberswald, *Feldzug 1712*, 136.
12 Villars, Barail, to Voisin, July 22, AG 2380.

in Marshal Montesquiou, his second in command, and Lieutenant General Puységur. No other person knew the plan. No courier carried advanced notice to Versailles. Quite to the contrary, Villars wrote the court that he had given up all thoughts of attacking Denain. All unit commanders received orders to prepare for a night march to relieve Landrecies at dawn.[13]

Lieutenant General Vieux-Pont led the advanced guard of thirty battalions and the bridge-building equipment supported by forty squadrons under Lieutenant General de Broglie. Major General Coigny received orders to harass the enemy around Landrecies with his thirty squadrons prior to the main attack. At the same time strong cavalry detachments were posted within sight of Bouchain and up and down the Seille to lessen the chance of a stray imperial patrol uncovering the ruse.[14]

At 5 P.M. on July 26 the advance guard of the Army of Flanders moved towards Landrecies. When the first units were five miles from camp, four brigades of infantry followed. Not until 9 P.M., when it was pitch dark, did the officers receive their final instructions. The imperial pickets must have seen the French advance and sent hard-riding couriers to Prince Eugene. The rapid march of the French showed that their baggage had been left behind—a sure sign of offering battle. The Army of Flanders had obviously marched out of camp with the common soldiers shouting for joy at going into action. But night had barely fallen when all units marched obliquely to the left, thereby completely missing the river. Were they just sneaking away and

13 Villars, De Broglie, D'Orval, July 23, AG 2380; duc de la Guiche, marquis of Goesbriand, July 23, AG A4, 8.

14 D'Orval, Villars, Contades, prince de Tingry, July 24, 25, AG 2380; Goesbriand, duc de la Guiche, July 24, 25, AG A4, 8; account by an unknown author, July 25, BN 20866; Eugene to the Emperor, Hensius, Zinzendorf, Royal Council of Spanish Netherlands, July 24, 25, in Eberswald, *Feldzug 1712*, 139, 140. The best secondary source for the combat at Denain is Maurice Sautai, *La Manoeuvre de Denain* (Lille, 1902). For other discussions, see bibliography.

leaving their bridges and baggage? A murmur of protest arose from the ranks. When Brigadier General Beaujou, who commanded at the bridgeheads, ordered the *Maison du Roi* to the left, the indignant junior officers cried out, "Are we not going to attack? Why are we being turned back?" It was with this sour disposition that the Army of Flanders marched away from its baggage and the completely fooled allies into a moonless night. But before very much ground had been covered, the true direction was quietly passed from unit to unit. The step quickened.

Villars, who was riding from column to column in a coach with Montesquiou, noted this change in humor with satisfaction. But his uneasiness had not abated. Here were five separate columns marching for one geographical point on a dark night. There would not be time to wait if any columns were late. By the early morning Prince Eugene would learn of the ruse and swing his entire army to the right. If the columns failed to reunite precisely on time, there was every possibility that the allies would be in a position to assault each column simultaneously in the front and the right flank. Such a result would spell disaster. The entire French army stood every chance of annihilation unless everything went perfectly.

Villars was counting on the advance guard crossing the Escaut before dawn. But at 5 A.M. a courier from De Broglie reported that the engineers were having difficulties constructing the bridges. From another rider Villars learned that one column had temporarily lost its way and would be at least one hour late. Members of the general staff began advising a general retreat while there was still time. Villars appeared to have decided to issue an order to halt the forward motion. At this point the Marshal Montesquiou intervened. Remarking that there was as yet no indication that the enemy had become informed, Montesquiou insisted that the columns should march at least as far as the

Escaut. Villars was not easily won over, feeling as he did that the element of surprise was gone. Montesquiou asked for permission to attack Denain with only the advance guard. At 7 A.M. the discussion was still going on when word arrived that the bridges were finished. Villars now decided to continue with the operation.

In the late hours of July 22 Prince Eugene wrote Emperor Charles VI that, by all the preliminary dispositions, Villars seemed resolved to go on the offensive to relieve Landrecies. Nevertheless Eugene intended to wait and see. Now, on the imperial side of the river, Eugene had seen the French battalions massing in the bend of the Escaut during his morning reconnaissance. But he still did not believe that Villars had any intention of trying to cross a river to attack as strongly fortified a position as Denain. Deciding that Villars would not be such a fool, Eugene went to breakfast.

In the camp of Lord Albermarle behind the entrenchment of Denain everything was perfectly tranquil. Most of the horses were out grazing and the soldiers were sitting around at breakfast. Only the French advance guard was across the Escaut at 8 A.M. when Major General Bothmar began his morning inspection of the works of Denain. To his amazement some thirty battalions of the French line were in full view with more racing across the bridges each second. Six cannon shots were fired, a courier left for Eugene's camp, the Dutch fusiliers answered the call to general quarters, and Bothmar rushed out with every available cavalryman in an attempt to delay the French.

Lieutenant General de Broglie's thirty squadrons, deployed on the plain before Denain, brushed aside the hastily collected, poorly formed cavalry of General Bothmar and fell on a 500-wagon supply convoy camped nearby. At this same time news reached Lord Albermarle that the fifth French column (from Valenciennes) was approaching from the north. The day was not yet lost for the allies, because the

swampy ground along the Escaut was slowing up the remainder of the French hurrying across the bridges. As each
unit crossed, Marshal Montesquiou placed it in line of battle.
But at 11 A.M., despite all efforts and several new bridges, one
column remained behind the Escaut.

Villars now had another attack of nerves. With his army
cut in two by the Escaut, the French position was exceedingly dangerous. Officers and men alike were anxiously
scanning the eastern horizon. Villars finally galloped into
the water and swam his horse across. But his charger slipped
on the swampy ground on the far bank, flinging Villars
violently to the ground, again wrenching his knee. Remount-
ing, the marshal was cheered by the shouts of the soldiers
of the regiments of Navarre and Champagne as they began
to cross the river in imitation of their general.

Finally alerted by Albermarle's courier, Prince Eugene
hastened with all his available cavalry towards Denain,
arriving just at midday. Seeing the French line arranged
in an attack formation that was growing larger by the minute, Eugene quickly gave orders for Albermarle to hold to
the last extremity and sent the seven battalions around
Thiant into Denain. Then Eugene rode back to hurry along
the imperial infantry. But the allied advanced foot guard
was still seven miles from the Escaut.

With the all-too-familiar standard on the horizon, the
time for Villars' final decision had arrived. Yet he hesitated.
Montesquiou rode up, and the two men walked aside and
engaged in an animated conversation. The contents of this
conversation were never recorded. We do know the result.
The leading forty battalions of the French line were massed
in fourteen lines at twenty-five pace intervals, preceded by
the grenadier companies. Twelve battalions were in reserve,
and the cannon were massed to the rear. Along the front of
the line rode the Marshal Montesquiou with Lieutenant
Generals Dreux, Vieux-Pont and Brendle. Where was Villars?

He says in his memoirs that he was on the right flank. But several eyewitnesses place him near the reserve watching the eastern horizon and hurrying the rest of the French infantry over the Escaut.

Montesquiou drew up his staff within the French formation. At his signal the French line advanced at the slow step, bayonets poised. For the Dutch fusiliers behind the entrenchments of Denain the sight before them must have been impressive, and perhaps frightening. Twenty-six thousand bayonets gleamed in the sun. Five hundred drums beat the step. Flags flapped hungrily in the crisp breeze. As the lines came closer, the Dutch could see the hard lines of determination etched on the faces of the French infantrymen. The French line approached closer and closer to the entrenchments and still not a single shot rang out. Only the deep roar of the opposing cannon could be heard. When a piece of round shot came plowing through the French ranks, scattering men like tenpins, the lines closed up without faltering. At fifty paces the leading ranks could hear the crisp commands from behind the entrenchments. "Ready! Sight!" At twenty paces the Dutch began firing from three revolving lines, while six pieces of artillery emitted the living hell of grapeshot. Within an instant 1,200 white-coated infantrymen were down. Of the leading three battalions not one man survived. But in the smoke the French infantrymen hurled themselves into the ditch fronting the entrenchments and began to climb up the other side. The Chevalier de Quincy reported that the men stood on each other's shoulders to get out of the trench. When the smoke cleared, the Dutch found themselves covered with a rapidly thickening mass of French infantrymen. Before such an onslaught the Dutch broke and ran in utter disorder. Vainly Lord Albermarle sought to rally his forces, until he was taken prisoner with hundreds of his men.

From his excellent observation point Prince Eugene was

powerless to aid his troops in Denain. When the imperial advance guard of fourteen battalions approached the Escaut, it was decimated by the French reserve led by Villars. And as he saw the garrison of Valenciennes approaching at the double, Eugene correctly judged the day lost and hastened to his headquarters.

In this engagement a powerful allied camp had fallen to the French Army of Flanders, at a cost of 2,016 killed and wounded, from a combination of unusual circumstances. Based upon the idea of a magistrate, a sound maneuver, Montesquiou's personal bravery, and a mistake in judgment, the fall of Denain was the turning point in the War of the Spanish Succession. The consequences of the victory soon surpassed the immediate exaltation of the court and the grim admiration of Prince Eugene. The Dutch were terrified at the thought that Villars had destroyed twenty-seven of their best battalions and had regained freedom of movement. The English subsidy was gone. Of more military significance, the Army of Flanders had cut Eugene's supply line squarely in two.[15]

Without losing even one hour, Villars took full advantage of the bewildered imperial army. Lieutenant General de Broglie marched to attack Marchiennes. Should that city be taken swiftly, Eugene's army would not have sufficient supplies to remain in the field. On July 30 Marchiennes capitulated. In the city the French found immense magazines of war which included one hundred new cannon, powder, shot, and clothing as well as bread, cheese, and grain. Eugene had no choice but to raise the siege of Landrecies and march north.[16]

To stop Eugene from reinforcing Douai, Villars proceeded at once to the siege of that city. As the investment

---

[15] Contades to Voisin, July 29, AG 2380, gives 880 dead and 1,136 wounded.
[16] Villars, D'Orval, Montesquiou, July 25-30, AG 2380; Goesbriand to duc du Maine, July 28, AG A4, 8; Eugene to the Emperor, July 31, in Eberswald, *Feldzug 1712*, 144; Villars to Louis XIV, July 31, AG 2380.

progressed, Villars attacked Fort de la Scarpe, which capitulated within three days. On September 8 Douai surrendered without conditions. One week later Villars was opening trenches before Quesnoy. Eugene had concentrated a large garrison with 116 pieces of large-caliber artillery in this city. The enemy garrison resisted vigorously, but a sortie failed on September 21 with large losses, and their fire had been reduced by two-thirds by September 26. Villars drew up three columns before the walls and announced that he would assault. The garrison commander opened negotiations which led to capitulation on October 3.[17]

Without losing one minute, Villars dispatched a corps to besiege Bouchain, which capitulated on October 19. In two months, the Army of Flanders had taken an entrenched camp, raised the siege of Landrecies, and retaken four cities. In sixty days the allied gains of two years had been wiped out. Without counting the usual trophies of war, some fifty-three battalions of the allied army had been destroyed or captured. Prince Eugene, entirely without supplies, could do nothing but retire to Brussels. The Netherlands, Portugal, and Savoy suddenly became more than ready to negotiate with Louis XIV at Utrecht. Only the Habsburgs and, because of them, the Empire remained implacable.[18]

The campaign of 1712 had certainly proven to be the most successful for France in the War of the Spanish Succession. It is possible that Villars displayed a lack of audacity and that his usual aggressiveness was missing in this campaign. There can be no doubt that a subtle change in the personality of Villars had taken place after Malplaquet. The years of constant defeat, the long-term effects of his crippling wound, and the solemn interview with Louis XIV seemed to convince Villars that he was no longer invincible. It is useless to argue whether or not the change

17 August 1-October 3, AG 2381, 2382, 2383, 2384, 2385; Eberswald, *Feldzug 1712*, August 3, 21, 28, September 12, 208ff.
18 Villars to Louis XIV, October 6, 9, AG 2385, 2386.

was temporary. For because of the results of Denain, the initiative returned to France. Villars was never again to be on the defensive. He was never again to lead a dispirited, defeated army. There can be no legitimate basis for comparison, as a victorious general whose forces far outnumber those of his adversary has little reason to exercise caution.

CHAPTER NINE

Shadow over the Empire, 1713

THROUGHOUT THE WINTER OF 1712-1713 THE CONGRESS
of Utrecht continued its deliberations. Faced by an apparent
Anglo-French truce, the other members of the grand alliance one by one left the war. When the provisions of many
separate treaties were combined and signed on April 11,
1713, as the Peace of Utrecht, only the Habsburgs and the
Holy Roman Empire remained at war with France. The representative of Charles VI had trumpeted at Utrecht that the
emperor would accept nothing less than the entire patrimony of the deceased Charles II of Spain. But the accords
with England, Holland, Portugal, Prussia, and Savoy had
reduced the theaters of war to one. For the first time in his
long reign Louis XIV would be able to concentrate an overwhelming force on the Rhine frontier. Contingents began
the long march toward Alsace from Spain, the Spanish Netherlands, and the southeast.

However, when Villars arrived in Metz on May 24 to take
command, the Army of the Rhine totaled only 45,000. Across
the Rhine, Prince Eugene had collected 60,000 men and was
fortifying the lines of Etlingen while awaiting the arrival
of contingents promised by many princes of the Empire.

This defensive posture on the part of the imperials surrendered the initiative to Villars, who moved quickly to
carry the terrible effects of offensive warfare into the Empire.
Villars' first objective was to recapture Landau, which in
imperial hands constituted a permanent menace to the
northern frontier of Alsace. The fall of this large fortress
would be of great political and military significance. Landau
had been taken by the Prince of Baden in 1702 and regained by Tallard in 1703, only to be lost during the debacle
of 1704. The first step of the operation would be to fix
the imperial positions on the far side of the Rhine in order
that the French lines of supply and communication from
Saarlouis, Strasbourg, and Metz would remain open.[1]

Employing a tactic in which he excelled, Villars moved
swiftly to dislodge the imperial garrisons along the east bank
of the Rhine. After starting a detachment towards the
Lauter, he crossed the Rhine on June 3 at the most unlikely
spot, the bridges of Strasbourg. A strong cavalry detachment swept towards Offenburg, as if to clear the approaches
to the Black Forest. On June 4 thirty French squadrons
appeared before Rastatt, openly reconnoitering the lines
of Ettlingen. On the same day forty battalions of the line
took the road from Strasbourg to Ettlingen but, after making
sure they had been seen, recrossed the Rhine on pontoon
bridges and marched for Lauterbourg. The area of concentration had been set at a geographical midpoint between
Saverne, Strasbourg, and Haguenau. All of these movements were executed with almost incredible speed, even
for a forced march. Some mounted units covered forty miles
in twenty-four hours. Alert and vigorous, despite his sixty
years and stiff leg, Villars galloped from column to column
encouraging his soldiers by his presence and his flag.

[1] Villars, Besons, Voisin, De Broglie, May 24-June 1, AG 2453, 2454; Eugene
to the Emperor, Swabian, Franconian, and Rhenish Circles, May 26, in
Ottokar Machalicky, *Spanischer Successions-Krieg, Feldzug 1713* (Vienna,
1892), 15; De Vogüé, *Mémoires*, III, 184ff.

The spectacle of French units marching in three directions gave Eugene no chance to counteract Villars' plan. All the Prince could do was to concentrate his available forces around Rastatt and wait for the situation to clear. On June 5 the French advance guard appeared before Speyer. The shocked Archbishop of Speyer arose from bed to find a marshal of France commandeering his personal apartment and the French general staff in his chapel. That same day French cavalry units descended on the small imperial strongpoints on the road to Philippsburg. Occupation of these two places cut Landau's line of communication with the right bank of the Rhine.

Partly to recompense his troops for their hard march, but also to give the impression that his real goal was Mannheim, Villars gave the city of Speyer to his rapacious soldiers for two days. But during this period of forty-eight hours, thirty French squadrons entrenched themselves on all the usual crossing points on the Rhine between Lauterbourg and Fort Louis. On the right bank of the Rhine a strong detachment took the road to Kaiserlautern, butchering the small imperial detachments between Mainz and Kaiserlautern. In the same two days, eighty French squadrons scoured the rich countryside of the Palatinate, collecting all available money and supplies useful to the army. Villars' siege corps of sixty-four battalions stood poised before Landau.[2]

Landau was probably the greatest example of Vauban's defensive art. The fortress consisted of many reinforced redoubts surrounding a double-starred cluster, protected by a large ditch which was seconded by a smaller wall, behind which an unusually strong covered wall provided a continuous parapet for musketry. Behind the main wall numerous demilunes and a covered redoubt insured com-

2 For movements to isolate Landau, see Villars to Voisin, June 2, AG 2454: Voisin, Villars, Louis XIV, June 5, 6, AG 2454; Machalicky, *Feldzug 1713*, 156-69; De Vogüé, *Mémoires*, III, 185-89.

munications with the citadel, itself a strong fortress situated on the highest point of land. Within this series of fortifications the capable, energetic Prince Charles of Württemburg commanded a garrison of 10,000 picked troops, with ample provisions and a large artillery park.[3]

After a preliminary reconnaissance with Lieutenant General Valory, his chief of engineers, Villars characteristically decided to reduce the most difficult cornered work of the exterior line of defense. The first trenches were opened on the night of June 24 with the siege corps nominally under the command of Marshal Besons. But the inability of Villars to remain idle or to move methodically in a war of position led him to supervise the works personally and to push the parallels rapidly to within fusil range. With this accomplished, despite a tremendous imperial counterbattery and large losses, the French infantry carried the works by frontal assault on July 3. Similarly on the night of July 4 the outer fort named Justice was overwhelmed. And on July 11 a fort named Alexander fell to the swarms of French infantry who scaled the covered wall and hacked the 300 defenders to pieces.[4]

The siege progressed in the same manner from July 12 to August 14. The constant pressure on several works prevented the Prince of Württemburg from concentrating a sufficiently large force at any one point to repel the ferocious bayonet attacks of the seemingly inexhaustible supply of French infantry. But the attacks were not made without serious losses, as the enemy, using all the skill of a slowly constricting defense, blew wide gaps in the charging battalions with mines and point-blank discharges of grapeshot. However, the determined Villars pressed on, and the golden fleur-de-lis of the Kingdom of France soon flew over the

[3] Eugene to Württemburg, February 20, Machalicky, *Feldzug 1713*, 7: physical description of Landau, see LIB #437 in the Bibliothèque de Guerre.
[4] Villars, Besons, Beslisle, Tressemane, June 9-July 12, AG 2454, 2455.

nine strongest outer works while the rapidly diminishing garrison grimly held on.[5]

During the night of August 15, a detachment of French grenadiers waded the outer moat and carried the small work of Malac, breaching the second defensive line. For thirty-six hours the grenadiers beat off the attempts of the garrison to dislodge them, despite little food and water and plunging fire from three sides. Despite their terrible losses, the French line sensed that the moment of triumph was at hand. On August 18 Villars personally led the wildly cheering French infantry to the attack of the principal bastion of the fortress. Discounting their rapidly mounting casualties, the French line scaled the wall and forced the garrison from two of the demilunes in fierce hand-to-hand combat.[6]

As soon as the gold and white of Bourbon flared over these two works, the cannon of the garrison fell silent. On the next day Prince Charles of Württemburg sounded the call to parlay while white flags appeared on the walls of the citadel. Villars met the imperial respresentatives in a small field nearby and insulted them by refusing to dismount. Always believing in intimidation, the marshal would not consider any terms other than unconditional surrender. The imperials quite naturally refused. The fortress replied as best it could for the next forty-eight hours. Once again the governor hoisted the white flag, and a mounted colonel approached Villars with a written capitulation. But since the imperials still demanded the honors of war, Villars only rode away. For the third time the French artillery began the bombardment, and the infantry returned to the assault. At every turn inside the walls, in every house, on every street, the decimated garrison did its utmost to hurl the

---

5 July 12-August 14, AG 2455; Eugene to the Emperor, July 14, 17, 31, August 31, to Württemburg, August 9, in Machalicky, *Feldzug 1713*, 162, 166, 193, 209, 213.

6 Villars to Voisin, August 18, AG 2456· Eugene to the Emperor, August 18, in Machalicky, *Feldzug 1713*, 233; De Vogüé, *Mémoires*, III, 200.

victorious army from the fortress. On August 20 the French infantry and dismounted cavalry were drawn up in long lines facing the fortress. Scaling ladders were everywhere. The French heavy siege guns rolled up hub to hub before the few remaining imperial strongpoints. Seeing these massive preparations for what would be the final assault, the weary, defeated Prince Charles of Württemburg personally surrendered the fortress to Villars unconditionally. On August 22 some 5,449 survivors entered captivity. The garrison had lost over 6,000 men while the French admitted 4,804 dead.[7]

It is difficult to assess the ability and valor of either the besieged or the French. The fortress had held out for fifty-six days against a combination of raw, blind attack and precision engineering work. Villars' method of siegecraft betrayed little concern for what is usually considered the eighteenth-century art of warfare or the amenities of current military practice. But whatever may have been the abilities of the various officers and soldiers concerned, Landau was once again French. Villars had been successful, and success is the only pawn of accountability on the field of battle.

While Lieutenant General Valory was on the way to Versailles with the forty-two flags and three standards of the defeated garrison, the Archbishop of Speyer ordered a Te Deum to honor the French victory, obviously paying court to the French garrison in his city. This one gesture on the part of a prince of the Holy Roman Empire signified that the long shadow of the Sun King again clouded the Habsburg horizon. Villars' dispositions for the siege had been so thorough that Prince Eugene had decided not to intervene, in the fervent hope that in his impatience his opponent would decimate the French army. But Louis XIV had poured

7 Villars, Besons, August 19, 20, 22, AG 2456; Villars to Maintenon, August 22, in Maintenon, *Lettres*, VII: Eugene to the Emperor, August 21, in Machalicky, *Feldzug 1713*, 237; Dangeau, *Journal*, XIV, 468.

reinforcements into the Army of the Rhine. Villars emerged from the siege of Landau commanding 200 full-strength battalions and 300 squadrons capable of further action.[8] Villars moved quickly to take full advantage of the fall of Landau. Squadrons were sent to harass the garrison of Mainz to keep the North German forces from marching south. The marshal had decided to march on Freiburg. Defended by a star fortress of eight bastions, which were in turn covered by three forts, all so placed as to facilitate enfilade fire on an attacking column, Freiburg occupied a position at the northen tip of the Black Forest which seemed impenetrable. The 13,000-man garrison was led by the Baron Harsch, an energetic commander whose stubbornness was to try Villars' patience severely. Prince Eugene judged Freiburg capable of repelling any attack at least until he could arrive with a relieving column. But to ensure doubly the safety of the imperial city, Eugene had dispatched fifteen battalions and twelve squadrons to patrol the banks of the Rhine and to cooperate with the garrison in the construction of very powerful outer defensive works on the heights of Roskopff and Hochgraben. But when a strong French detachment appeared before Karlsruhe and began to construct a bridge across the Rhine, Eugene was convinced that Villars was deploying for an attack on the lines of Ettlingen. Recalling all his forward units between Philippsburg and Mainz and along the Rhine, Eugene prepared to resist the French. At the same time, the Prince sent twenty squadrons to defend the passes of the Black Forest against some French dragoons sighted in the valley of the Hornberg.[9]

8 For an excellent exposition of Eugene's thoughts during the siege of Landau, see Machalicky, *Feldzug 1713*, 170-203; Villars to Louis XIV, September 7, AG 2457; gradual build-up of Villars' army, see AG A4, IX, 20.

9 Villars to Voisin, June 26, AG 2454; Voisin to Villars, July 17, AG 2455; Villars' plan of attack on Freiburg, AG 2457, 8; Voisin to Villars, September 13, AG 2457; Villars to Voisin, September 14, AG 2457; Eugene to Harsch, Vauboune, August 22, 23, to the Emperor, September 9, 11, 15, in Machalicky, *Feldzug 1713*, 243, 245, 268, 282, 289.

When the excellent French cavalry reported the withdrawal of the imperial screen along the Rhine, Villars moved. On September 16 the advance guard of thirty battalions crossed the Rhine at Kehl and marched for Freiburg. That same evening Villars gave a grand military ball at Strasbourg, openly bragging that he would soon be marching to chase Eugene from Ettlingen. In the very early hours of the seventeenth he mounted his horse to rejoin the army. The French troops were kept marching until the evening of the eighteenth, having covered forty-five miles. By September 21 Villars camped at the foot of the imperial strongpoint of Roskopff in full view of Freiburg.[10]

At daybreak Villars brushed aside the fears of the Count of Bourg, who warned that there had not been time to cut sufficient brush to fill the ditch, by saying that the bodies of the first line would do very nicely. With that, the French flanks swept around the small fort while the French center literally jumped into the dry ditch and scaled the opposite earthen wall, sweeping aside the defenders in a matter of minutes. From Roskopff the fire of the French fusiliers raked the parapets of Hochgraben, making them untenable. In its turn, Hochgraben surrendered, and the neighboring smaller works were evacuated by the enemy.[11]

The first set of parallels was opened on September 30, but due to the effective counterthrusts of the garrison it was not until October 2 that the siege battery of twenty-eight pieces of 24-pound cannon could open fire. Here again Villars practiced his principle of intimidation. Several of the guns were fired directly into the city, causing great alarm and many casualties among the civilian population. On October 7, 8, and 9 the assaults of the French infantry

[10] Beauville, De Broglie, Contades, Asfeld, Montevel, Villars to Voisin, September 16, 17, 18, 20, 23, AG 2457; Eugene to the Emperor, September 18, in Machalicky, *Feldzug 1713*, 296.

[11] Villars, Contades, Le Guerchois, Asfeld, to Voisin, September 21, 22. AG 2457.

were repulsed with heavy losses. Villars tried a night attack, but the ground blew up in the faces of the French grenadiers when the garrison exploded several large mines. During a driving rainstorm, on the night of October 13, the marshal sent forty companies of grenadiers against one of the lunettes of the covered wall. But at that same moment some 2,100 of the garrison counterattacked. There resulted one of those nightmarish, confused bayonet attacks in which friend is indistinguishable from foe. The loss on both sides must have been large, as the French admitted to 1,200 dead.[12]

The first snowfall of the season, on October 16, filled Villars with apprehension. Despite some progress in reducing the fortress, the garrison seemed full of fight, and his losses had been extremely heavy. But by good fortune, and possibly because they sensed another victory, the French soldiers were not disheartened. To add to his fears, Villars learned that 30,000 imperials were approaching Hochgraben. He detached thirty battalions to contain them, but after remaining in full view of the French army for twenty-four hours, the imperials withdrew. Delivered from any fear of a flank attack, Villars decided to finish the siege. On October 19 six new batteries of heavy siege artillery began firing directly into the city with terrifying effect. The bombardment was constant for six days and nights without a minute's respite. One part of the main wall crumbled, and Villars fixed November 2 for a sweeping general assault. Dawn on the second found the French infantry drawn up in columns before the breach. At that moment the white flag was hoisted over the breach, and the magistrates of Freiburg came forth to yield the city.[13]

12 Villars, Valory, Contades, Houssaye, to Voisin, October 1-10, AG 2458; Anger to Villars, October 15, AG A4, IX, #2, 18; Dangeau, *Journal*, XI, 2ff, 9, 10.

13 Villars to Voisin, October 10, 30, AG 2458, 2459; Beslisle to unknown, October 20, AG A4, IX, #2; Anger to unknown, November 1, AG A4, IX, #2.

As usual Villars met the representatives of the defeated on horseback and demanded a payment of one million livres for permitting them to surrender. After the reluctant magistrates agreed, Villars sent a message to Harsch, whom he secretly admired, that the French army would shortly be occupying the city of Freiburg. If just one French soldier should be hurt by any action of the garrison, he, Villars, would butcher the entire population. If Harsch wished, he might surrender with the honors of war. The baron replied that he had no authority to surrender the citadel. Only Prince Eugene could do that. Villars told Harsch to dispatch a courier to the prince for permission. Two horsemen left immediately.[14]

Villars quickly cut the 5,000 men in the citadel off from the outside world and warned Harsch that the army of the king would live off the city and that any consequences for the imperial wounded and the citizens of Freiburg would be charged to the prolonged defense. In a moving reply, Baron Harsch stated that his honor forbade surrender and that he did not believe that any representative of the Most Christian King would be capable of maltreating wounded prisoners and defenseless civilians. Villars answered that neither his honor nor his religion would permit him to give subsistence to anyone who shot or aided in the shooting of French soldiers. As a result, either Baron Harsch could feed the wounded and the people or he could watch them slowly starve to death.[15]

At this same time Villars took hostages from among the leading citizens of Freiburg to ensure the conduct of the civilian population, and not one piece of bread was issued to the people or the imperial wounded. When two days

[14] Harsch to Eugene, November 2, in Alfred R. von Arneth, *Prinz Eugen von Savonen* (Vienna, 1864), II, 507; Eugene to the Emperor, November 6, in Machalicky, *Feldzug 1713*, 390; Villars, Houssaye, November 1, 3, AG 2460; De Vogüé, *Mémoires*, III, 228.

[15] Harsch, Villars, November 4, 6, AG 2460; De Vogüé, *Mémoires*, III, 228ff.

passed and Harsch still refused to yield, Villars resorted to an extreme measure. Under a flag of truce, twenty of the most seriously wounded imperials were abandoned before the drawbridge of the citadel. Now Villars massed sixty cannon and many infantry battalions behind these unfortunate wretches. A note reached the startled Harsch stating that unless he surrendered within twenty-four hours the citadel and the town would be destroyed. On November 16 Harsch, convinced that Villars meant his every word, capitulated. As a mark of his satisfaction with Baron Harsch's conduct, Villars permitted the garrison the full honors of war. The total survivors of the garrison, including wounded, did not number 6,000.[16]

There is no way of knowing whether or not Villars would have carried his threats to their logical conclusions. But it is contended that he would have done exactly what he threatened to do. With snow covering the ground and the army weakened by tremendous efforts, Villars would have courted military disaster if he had failed to take Freiburg. The marshal never believed that war was a gentleman's game or mere child's play as did many in the eighteenth century. War for him meant conquest in the name of the king. Moral objections and religious plumage had no place on the battlefield. Villars believed, as have all great captains, that the primary objective in a war is to destroy, by any and all means available, the will of the enemy to resist.

The sledgehammer blows of the Army of the Rhine during the campaign of 1713 disheartened Emperor Charles VI, who had expected that he would celebrate the new year in Paris after his army was victorious on the Rhine. On August 24 Villars had received word that he had been designated as Louis XIV's principal negotiator in a forth-

16 Eugene to Harsch, November 6, 13, 14, in Machalicky, *Feldzug 1713*, 392, 394, 397; Villars, November 10, 13, 15, 17, to Voisin and Louis XIV, AG 2460; the best two continuous accounts of the siege will be found in Machalicky, *Feldzug 1713*, 317-89, and AG, *Mémoires historiques*, #93.

coming peace conference with the Holy Roman Empire. The credentials stated the minimum settlement that Louis XIV would consider. Bitche, Homburg, and Freiburg would be returned; but either Philippsburg, or Brisach, or Kehl would be retained. The Electors of Cologne and Bavaria were to be reinstated in all their dignities and possessions. Nothing else anywhere was negotiable. In transmitting these instructions, the Marquis of Torcy noted that peace was essential. Since Emperor Charles VI had designated Prince Eugene as his representative, the friendly enemies would now face each other over the conference table.[17]

Villars received from Prince Eugene, on November 20, a message that requested his presence at Rastatt to open the peace talks. When all the details were arranged, Villars wrote Louis XIV, on his day of departure, that he dared to believe that after serving so many years in the army with distinction he would now conclude a peace which would radiate the piety and justice of the king. When Villars stepped into his carriage with a light, happy heart, he did not know that the next five months would be among the most trying in his life.[18]

---

[17] Louis XIV to Villars, *Correspondance politique*, Archives de la Ministère des Affaires Étrangers (hereinafter cited as AAE, *CP*), August 24.
[18] Eugene to Villars, November 21, AG 2460.

CHAPTER TEN

A Midnight Bargain, 1713-1714

VILLARS ARRIVED AT THE CASTLE OF RASTATT ON NOVEM-
ber 26, 1713, less than one-half hour before his imperial
counterpart. When the escort of Prince Eugene appeared
with drums beating and trumpets blowing, Villars, leaning
heavily on his cane, hobbled to the top of the front steps.
An aide hurried forward with the marshal's apologies for
not descending the staircase but it would be improper for a
representative of the "Very Christian Monarch" to be carried
in an official ceremony. While the French and Austrian
honor guards lined up on their respective sides of the court-
yards, Eugene climbed the steps and embraced the marshal.
The affection was returned. Leaving to aides-de-camp all
the necessary formalities, the two men retired for a few hours
to relive the great Hungarian campaign that had culmin-
ated in the Battle of Zenta (1697), in which Eugene had
smashed the Turks.[1]

These pleasant reminiscences were terminated as they
quickly returned to business and both men retired to their
apartments for the first formal protocol meetings. Villars,
as the guest, visited the prince in his apartment for fifteen
minutes. One-half hour later, Eugene returned the call.

The generals-diplomat decided to spend their days together and to discuss the problems of peace or war in one long session each evening. With what appeared to be an excellent rapport established, Villars wrote that he was with the greatest difficulty controlling his natural optimism and that he could hold out great hope that the "drums would never again sound assembly in this war."[2]

The inner feelings of Prince Eugene were far different. The celebrated prince of Savoy was a discouraged man who could conceal only with the utmost difficulty the pain of defeat that lay just below the surface of his gray exterior. All his genius, all his efforts had been in vain. Undoubtedly Eugene wished that the Habsburgs had negotiated a peace in 1710, as he had advised, when everything was in their favor. The prince had come to Rastatt with the full knowledge that, even if he obtained the very reasonable demands of Emperor Charles VI, Vienna would still remain unsatisfied unless the empire of Charles V was reconstituted. Eugene also feared that unless he negotiated a peace the French would quickly overrun much of the Empire. The refusal of many German princes to send their contingents to Ettlingen in 1713 had kept Eugene from the field. Now there was open discussion of a treaty of peace, with or without the emperor. However, this grave and unhappy prince let not one hint of his true feelings come to the surface. Villars and Louis XIV were never to doubt the emperor's ability to continue the war.

At the first official session Marshal Villars presented the *sine qua non* conditions of Louis XIV. Landau would remain in French hands. Freiburg would be returned only if suitable compensation was forthcoming. The Electors of Bavaria and Cologne were to be returned to all their estates and privileges and would be paid an adequate compensation

---

1 Villars to Voisin, November 27, AG 2460; Eugene to the Emperor, November 27, in Machalicky, *Feldzug 1713*, 415.
2 *Ibid.*

for their material losses by the Diet of the Holy Roman Empire. As for all the rest, on the numerous points that appeared as secondary considerations to Versailles, Villars was authorized to take the most expedient course to facilitate an early peace. Hardly had he finished reading when Eugene jumped to his feet declaring that the French claims were impossible, unjustified, and unacceptable. With his temper and voice climbing on each phrase, he shouted that he had believed that the French king desired peace. But apparently that monarch only wished to gain time in order to replenish his badly crippled army. To cap his performance, Eugene jammed on his hat and majestically marched out of the room.[3]

Villars sat quietly for some minutes in a state of semi-shock. Then as he slowly and heavily limped from the room he could not conceal his great disappointment from the imperial aides who were still present. He wrote that he had not expected a rupture so quickly. But the heavy scrawl of this letter becomes a thin line of excitement as Villars announces that he has been interrupted by Eugene's aide-de-camp, who has asked for a copy of the French demands. The prince has agreed to send a report on the French position to Vienna and await instructions. The letter concludes on a note of hopeful expectancy.[4]

Villars was handed the Austrian demands on December 3. The Emperor Charles VI required the restitution of the Peace of Ryswick, which would return Kehl, Freiburg, and Landau to imperial control. Naples, Sicily and the Spanish Netherlands were to become Austrian. If France would agree to the above stipulations the emperor would recommend the reestablishment of the Electors of Cologne and Bavaria to the Diet of the Holy Roman Empire. These con-

3 Louis XIV to Villars, AAE, *CP*, 92, 186-207; Villars to Voisin, November 30, AG 2560; Anquetil, *Villars*, II, 298ff.
4 Villars to Voisin, November 30, AG 2460; Ernest Moret, *Quinze ans du regne de Louis XIV* (Paris, 1859), III, 308.

ditions were so completely different from those of the French that a permanent rupture of the negotiations seemed inevitable. The official conferences now became formal and rigid. From these rather sterile sessions came Villars' proposal of December 5 that if Louis XIV would content himself with Landau and the terms of the Peace of Ryswick there would be a faint hope for peace. In this case the open and impulsive Villars miscalculated the haughty, cold poise of Eugene. The prince used a gambit to the best possible gain for his emperor. Every time Villars so much as raised his voice, Eugene threatened to end the negotiations. Quite a spectacle! For once Villars had found a man he could not bully.[5]

At Versailles Louis XIV was not fooled by this display of Latin temper or by his marshal's customary haste. The Marquis of Torcy, Secretary of State for Foreign Affairs, advised Villars on December 7 and December 9 that the king was aware of the emperor's demands and had read the wild rantings of a prince who acted as if all the advantages of war were on his side. The plenipotentiary of the king of France was not to lose sight of the advantages of war possessed by France. After all, the French had been invited to Rastatt. Louis XIV had every intention of retaining Freiburg as a heavily fortified city unless suitable compensations were forthcoming. As for the restoration of the Electors of Bavaria and Cologne, that was not a matter for negotiation. The secretary closed by reminding Villars that any treaty which did not embody these conditions was totally unacceptable.[6]

To emphasize his wishes, Louis XIV wrote that although he desired peace there was absolutely no one who could

5 Villars to Voisin, December 3, 5, AG 2461; Villars to Louis XIV, December 3, 5, AAE, *CP,* 94; Villars to Torcy, AAE, *CP,* 94, 61, 62.

6 Torcy to Villars, December 7, 9, AAE, *CP,* 94: decisions of Louis XIV on the imperial demands of December 3, 7, AAE, *CP,* 94.

force an undesirable treaty upon him. If Villars wished to continue as his representative, he must demonstrate more firmness. If Eugene were to break off negotiations, the king would applaud Villars.[7]

With his hand strengthened and his thinking somewhat straightened out, Villars presented Eugene with a resume of the king's and the secretary's letters. But the prince must have seen some latent uncertainty in the marshal's manner, as he persisted in his negative attitude. Villars actually fled from the conference room to pen a dispatch saying that Eugene would refuse the king's terms even if the French army were in Linz and that he should leave Rastatt as all was lost. In this same hour of mental torment, he wrote Louis XIV that he had failed miserably.[8]

At a second session late that night, Villars learned that the most unacceptable point of the French position was the compensation demand on behalf of the Elector of Bavaria. Charles VI thought that the Elector of Cologne had had very little choice, but it was impossible to offer a monetary compensation to the Elector of Bavaria. There certainly was no precedent in all the annals of the Empire for the Diet to reward a prince for disloyalty. Eugene concluded by saying that perhaps the king of France did not really want peace. Villars attempted to reply by intimating that the Empire was incapable of another campaign. Enraged, Eugene leaped to his feet and shouted at the top of his voice, "Your king is mistaken if he believes that the Empire is defeated by the loss of two cities! We are preparing a new campaign at this very moment!" Then the prince lowered his voice and injected a very slight pleading quality, "Why is it that we cannot find a way to peace, whose fruits are so sweet? Assuredly if we two are not successful, peace will be

7 Louis XIV to Villars, December 7, 9, AAE, *CP*, 94.
8 Villars to Louis XIV, December 9, AG 2461; Villars to Louis XIV, December 11, AAE, *CP*, 94.

a long time in coming. But the excessive demands of your king that my emperor considers injurious make peace impossible. I cannot do anything but leave."[9]

Villars actually pleaded with the prince, who finally consented to think the matter over. On the very next day, December 18, Eugene announced that out of consideration for the damage that might be done to the marshal's reputation he would stay another eight days. But he would accord this delay only if a courier were dispatched to Versailles for new instructions immediately. Villars ended his account of this rather extraordinary series of events by begging Louis XIV to lessen his "excessive" demands lest the negotiations end. Prince Eugene had indeed read correctly the mobile face of his opponent.[10]

Although not mesmerized for a moment by the strutting attitude of Prince Eugene, Louis XIV did genuinely desire peace. Louis XIV agreed to pay Max Emmanuel of Bavaria two million livres to cover his personal losses. But when replying to Villars' panic, the king stated that if there was to be peace the Electors of Bavaria and Cologne would be reestablished in all their lands, titles, and dignities and the terms of the Peace of Ryswick would be enforced, with the exception that Landau must remain French. This letter proved to be acceptable to Charles VI. Only one other major question remained to be solved—adequate compensation for the return of Freiburg.[11]

During the negotiations the Elector of the Palatinate had secretly suggested to Villars that he would be willing to sacrifice the strategic district of Gemersheim for the return of Freiburg to the emperor if such a trade would hasten the

9 Villars to Louis XIV, December 14, AAE, CP, 94; Villars to Voisin, December 14, AG 2461; Villars to Louis XIV, December 16, AG 2461.

10 Villars to Torcy, December 17, 18, AAE, CP, 94; Villars to Louis XIV, December 16, 18, AG 2461; Villars to Louis XIV, December 18, AAE, CP, 94.

11 Louis XIV to Villars, December 22, AAE, CP, 94; Torcy to Villars, AAE, CP, 94.

peace. Louis XIV agreed. But when Villars proposed the idea to Eugene, the prince cried, "There is another mistake of your ministers. At this moment when all the difficulties seemed resolved, they think of this. They do not want peace. They want war. Well, they shall have it. Never would my Lord, the Emperor, consent to French possession of any of Germany's soil!"[12]

As Villars reported to Louis XIV, the negotiations had again reached a stalemate. But on December 29, at 10 P.M., Eugene called on the marshal. A long night session ensued during which Eugene argued that the war would begin again, with Villars responding that the Circles were incapable of furnishing subsidies or manpower to continue the war. Eugene smilingly informed Villars, "You are wrong, Sir, the German Diet has just voted five million florins for war purposes." Apparently this statement completely unnerved Villars as he only lowered his head in silence. But the following day, Eugene was surprised to find him in a cheerful mood and asked the reason for it. Villars, carefully keeping to himself that he had at last seen through the prince's diplomacy, only replied that he would rather have the war continue. "After all, the army of the king will be operating on enemy soil and I will cover myself with glory and enrich myself at the emperor's expense." The baffled prince hastily assured Villars that he was negotiating in good faith and that the emperor really desired peace. Eugene's threats of disrupting the negotiations ceased at that moment.[13]

Despite the return to a personal equilibrium, the embarrassment of the two negotiators must have been extreme. They were now faced with intransigency in both Vienna and Versailles. But on his own initiative Villars offered to

12 Louis XIV to Villars, December 22, AAE, *CP*, 94; Villars to Louis XIV, Voisin, December 24, 29, AG 2461.
13 Villars to Louis XIV, Voisin, December 31, AG 2461; Arneth, *Prinz Eugen*, II, 310-39, gives an excellent discussion of Eugene's diplomatic style but unfortunately lacked access to Villars' correspondence.

surrender Freiburg without any compensation. A treaty was pieced together, and Villars was exuberant as he wrote that he had made a good and lasting peace. A letter to Louis XIV bragged that he had won the last battle. But for the second time Villars had misjudged the king. Torcy wrote on January 22 that Villars' treaty was only a tentative draft and that the king refused all but five articles. The real objection lay in the loose wording of many of the articles. The diplomatic staff at Versailles was rewriting the treaty and he, Villars, was to ensure Austrian acceptance. This pronouncement plunged Villars into the deepest gloom. Not only did he see disgrace for his diplomacy but a campaign pending for his tired and woefully unprepared army. A letter from Voisin did not help any. The minister of war foresaw a rupture of the peace talks and suggested that Villars order Lieutenant General de Broglie to assemble a large body of troops for an attack on the lines of Ettlingen before the imperials could prepare their resistance.[14]

Villars characteristically shook off his doldrums by becoming infuriated. In a letter to Louis XIV he demanded permission to return to Paris where he might confront the "creatures" who wished to prolong the war for their own benefit. At this same time Eugene was having his own troubles with the courtiers at Vienna who considered that he had yielded far more than was necessary. As Villars was not uninformed of the prince's difficulties, he approached Eugene and said, "You have your enemies in Vienna, Sir, and I have mine at Versailles."[15]

With both monarchs seemingly unwilling to allow a compromise, the negotiators began to pack. But Villars received a direct order from Louis XIV, saying: "If Prince Eugene threatens to leave, do nothing to detain him. If he does leave

[14] Villars, Voisin, January 2, 7, 10, 14, 22, AG 2506; Louis XIV, Villars, Torcy, January 3, 7, 22, AAE, CP, 94, 96.
[15] Villars to Louis XIV, January 28, February 2, AG 2506.

—you leave. If he stays—you stay. I will not be the first to break off negotiations."[16]

In a situation which now appeared hopeless, Eugene and Villars, driven by a genuine desire for peace and hatred for their respective courts, decided to try one last thing. Eugene gave a memoir in his own hand to Villars which totally exposed his instructions and the bare minimum acceptable to Vienna. Did Villars also pass over such valuable information? Possibly he did, but the documents are silent on this point. By mutual consent couriers left for Versailles and Vienna. Together the old friends hammered out a treaty which consisted only of points agreed upon while totally ignoring the questions of the succession to the Spanish throne and the Catalan problem. The next morning, on February 6, 1714, Villars left for Strasbourg and Eugene for Stuttgart after agreeing to return when word was received from their respective monarchs. On the same day Major General Contades, trusted friend and advisor of Villars, left for Versailles with the official treaty.[17]

On his arrival at court, Contades was ushered directly to the king's cabinet. There he had long sessions with Voisin, Torcy, and Louis XIV. Torcy soon wrote Villars that the king still objected to a few minor points on which he forbade further concessions. From Strasbourg Villars replied that he intended to remain in that delightful city. He was tired. His knee was hurting. Besides he would never be able to satisfy all the absurd longings of the court. At any rate he was convinced that the peace was advantageous and that the emperor would accept it. He simply would do no more. Realizing that the temperamental marshal had been pushed once too often, Torcy wrote to salve Villars' ruffled ego, saying that all Versailles was singing his praises; the

[16] Louis XIV to Villars, February 1, AAE, *CP*, 96.
[17] Eugene to Villars, February 6, AAE, *CP*, 96; Villars to Louis XIV, Voisin, February 6, 8, AG 2506.

marshal should not worry about the mutterings of those without official capacity; the king was indeed pleased with Villars. It is quite clear that Villars was referring to the king and that Torcy was well aware of that fact.[18]

This exchange did not please Louis XIV, who had had about all of Villars' impertinence that he would tolerate. The king charged Contades with the mission of seeking out Prince Eugene at Stuttgart and adjusting the remaining minor differences. Carrying precise instructions, which he was careful to reveal to Villars at Strasbourg, Contades arrived at Stuttgart on February 23, 1714. As Eugene explained in a letter announcing his arrival at Rastatt, Contades was charming, eloquent, gracious, and persuasive. Just a touch of final irony may be noted in the phraseology of this letter.[19]

On February 29 the two conspirators met at Rastatt. After congratulating themselves they approached the final act. Although most treaties were written in Latin, Villars knew only French and threatened a rupture unless the treaty was in his native tongue. Eugene, undoubtedly exasperated at this last sign of his colleague's temperament, agreed only after stipulating a final article which read that the use of French was not to be taken as a precedent.[20]

Finally on March 7, 1714, after a lengthy, formal reading to all members of both contingents assembled in the courtyard, during which the negotiators displayed increasing signs of boredom, Villars and Eugene signed the document. Then all assembled retired to a feast and entertainment that lasted throughout the night. Several days later Villars

18 Dangeau, *Journal*, XV, 80; Villars to Count of Lyonne, February 19, BN 20865 (fragment: only the first paragraph has survived); Torcy, Villars, February 15, 20, AAE, *CP*, 96, 97; Villars to Voisin, Louis XIV, February 20, 21, AG 2506.

19 Villars, Louis XIV, February 22, 23, 25, AAE, *CP*, 97, 99; Eugene, Louis XIV, Villars, February 23, 25, AG 2506; memoir of the changes demanded by Louis XIV, AG 2506, 156.

20 Villars to Voisin, Louis XIV, February 28, March 1, 4, 6, AG 2506.

reached Versailles where the king presented him an olive branch and granted him free access to the royal apartments at any time of the day or night. Then the monarch invited Villars to join him in the royal chapel where the Te Deum would very shortly be sung in celebration of the peace.[21]

Thus was peace restored to a Europe weary with thirteen years of cannon fire. Two generals had met to negotiate a peace. After finding their best attempts frustrated by the inability of their respective monarchs to compromise, they seemingly conspired to win the peace. It appears that Prince Eugene had undoubtedly given away an imperial secret by informing Villars of the exact text of his instructions. It is illogical and unbelievable in the circumstances surrounding the conference of February 5-6, 1714, to assume that Villars did not expose Louis XIV's position. There can also be little doubt that peace would have come soon whatever the results at Rastatt. Neither France nor the Empire was really capable of waging a decisive war by 1714. But Eugene and Villars were primarily soldiers. The genuine desire for peace on the parts of Charles VI and Louis XIV had far more to do with the conclusion of the War of the Spanish Succession than did the diplomatic abilities of the negotiators. Both courts were actually immensely satisfied with the results of February 5-6. At least Versailles knew of Eugene's exposure, and there is no reason to assume that Vienna did not know of Villars'. But was the opposite also known in both courts? The documents are silent.

21 Moret, *Quinze ans*, III, 311-14.

CHAPTER ELEVEN

Then Who Was Villars?

THE PRECEDING CHAPTERS HAVE RELATED THE STORY OF
France's fortunes in the War of the Spanish Succession, as
seen in the career of her most outstanding warrior. The
War of the Spanish Succession was actually a part of a world-
wide conflict that involved not only the powers of western
Europe, which had been instrumental in the establishment
of the Westphalia settlement, but also their vast colonial
possessions and the emerging powers to the south and east.
The contemporary Great Northern War (1700-1721) saw the
end of Swedish hegemony in the Baltic-Polish areas and
the meteoric rise of Russia under the tutelage of Peter the
Great. These two wars, complicated by the colonial aspects
of the struggle, saw the breakup of the Franco-Swedish alliance. That the two wars never actually merged can be
accounted for only by France's weakness, Charles XII's
youthful brashness, and possibly the eloquence of the Duke
of Marlborough during his 1707 audience with the Swedish
monarch.

Thus, by the time the treaties of Utrecht (1713) and
Rastatt-Baden (1714), generally grouped together under

the name of the Peace of Utrecht, were signed, several changes had radically altered the alignment of Europe and indeed the world. It is possible to denounce the Peace of Utrecht with the same fervor as some have the Treaty of Vienna (1815) and the Treaty of Versailles (1919). But these denunciations must be directed more to the particular interests of the nations concerned than to the effects on the general welfare of Europe. To institute secret negotiations for a private peace was a proceeding unworthy of England. To leave the Catalans and the Camisards to their fates at the hands of Philip V and Louis XIV was a serious blunder on the part of the allies. To permit Philip V to retain the crown of Spain and France to keep Alsace was unfair to the House of Habsburg (the one power which had consistently opposed French claims to European supremacy).

Yet from the European point of view the Peace of Utrecht merely registered accomplished facts. Since the general settlement at Westphalia (1648), several important changes had altered the order of things. France had become the leading nation of Europe. England (by 1715) had launched her career of colonial and commercial ascendancy, which was to make her the most powerful maritime country in the world. She was learning to found her colonial empire more upon military conquest than upon emigration. The cessions in North America were the beginnings of her hold over the vast stretches of the continent north of her seaboard colonies. The monopoly of the slave trade accorded England soon afforded further opportunities to penetrate the Spanish colonial empire. The dismemberment of the Holy Roman Empire had finally removed the last signs of nationalism and national policies from Germany. The smaller German states henceforth began to assemble around the largest powers in the north and south—Prussia and Austria. The "German Question" may be said to have begun. Furthermore, the cession of the western Milanese to the Duke of Savoy opened the door to the development of Italian unity.

It is generally accepted by European scholars that seventeenth-century history ends with the Peace of Utrecht. The attempt of France to establish a virtual hegemony over Europe had failed. France was to continue among the European nations—but no longer to be the predominant power. By 1715 the determination of England to attain commercial leadership, the effort of Prussia for international recognition, and the Austrian desires to regain Hungary and secure a footing in Italy were successful. By the treaties of Passarowitz (1718) and Nystadt (1721), which were to follow the Peace of Utrecht as surely as the treaties of Olivia and the Pyrenees had followed the Peace of Westphalia, Poland and Sweden surrendered eastern and northern European leadership to Russia and Prussia, while in the south Turkey alone barred Russia's path to the Pruth and the Black Sea. The stage was set with the cast in their positions for the first act of the eighteenth century which eventually led to the Congress of Vienna and beyond.

Many summaries have been written of the effect of the War of the Spanish Succession on France. It has become trite to say that France was a wealthy, flourishing nation when Louis XIV began his personal rule and that by 1715 French economic life was moribund and that the French people were faced with little hope that the pressing social reforms would be accomplished.

Certainly a weighty reason for these conditions lay in the long, exhausting warfare of Louis' reign. In 1715 France was internally weakened to the point of bankruptcy and externally confined by the new European balance of power. The creation of this balance involving all the states of Europe, which weakened Habsburg-French supremacy and which resulted in colonization throughout the world, was the final result of the French bid for European supremacy.

The social and economic effect of the War of the Spanish Succession for France was the partial ruin of the state. It is almost unbelievable that a country so completely prostrate by the spring of 1709 could emerge from the War of the Spanish Succession with even a draw. It is obvious that every fiber of France was strained beyond the normal breaking point for the maintenance of the royal army. The fact that, when things looked blackest and this army was staggering in defeat, France was able to obtain a draw in battle (as at Malplaquet in 1709) is amazing in itself. The story of this seemingly miraculous recovery on the field of honor actually lay in the personality and talents of one individual. Not Louis XIV, not the boasted French infantryman, but a man of scant previous military reputation must be given the credit—Claude Louis Hector, le maréchal de Villars.

How did this man from a very uninfluential segment of the new nobility of the Bourbon monarchy who lacked the advantage of wealth rise to become a marshal of France and the foremost general of the War of the Spanish Succession? The answer to this question lies in two things. In the first place Villars was consumed with ambition and determination to become a marshal. We have seen that he succeeded. Secondly, Villars was loyal to the House of Bourbon. At times the reader may suspect that Villars might subconsciously be repaying Louis XIV for some of the slights of his earlier years. Such was not the case. Villars was one of those rare individuals who believed in his own ability so strongly that he had sufficient courage to defy the all-powerful monarch in ways that had led many others to the block or to decay in isolation on rundown country estates. It is a mark of his confidence that Villars was able successfully to defy the king and to be proven right by the fortunes of war.

This self-sufficiency unmasks the principal feature of

Villars' personality and also accounts for his attitude towards both subordinates and superiors. One set of important relationships of any general are those with his fellow officers and his enlisted men. The enlisted men, in a word, loved Villars. He was the only winning general they had. No soldier prefers to run away or to retreat constantly, year after year, or to be defeated, time and time again, because of incompetence at the top. Villars could be counted upon by the enlisted ranks to give them a better than even chance of winning. Also, he was noted for his willingness to share their hardships, for his good humor, and for his ability to stand up to those who would or could not furnish them with the necessities of war. This relationship cannot be defined—it can only be stated in two words, mutual confidence.

Villars' officers, on the other hand, must have constantly tottered on the edge of desperation. True, Villars did not demand anything of them that he had not already done, but the demands to die at one's post, no quarter for the enemy, sacking, and constant exposure to enemy fire were often carried to the extreme. Therefore it is not surprising that the subordinate officers either hated or loved him. The two lieutenant generals who threw themselves in front of Villars at Malplaquet certainly loved him. One paid for his devotion with an arm, the other with his life. The officers who informed on Villars in the 1703 Bavarian campaign and those prosecuted for incompetence in 1708 are examples of those who hated him. Apparently Villars' thinking with his subordinate officers went something like this. If you are competent and carry out every order with a satisfactory spark of initiative, you are in line for promotion. But should you show the slightest hesitation, especially under fire, or attempt to win favor by a courtier's methods, you are in line for degradation. To his senior officers Villars gave nothing but contempt. No matter how he might laugh with Boufflers or Vendôme, Villars always believed that he was the only competent marshal and made no attempt to hide his feelings.

Villars went so far as to treat Louis XIV, Chamillart, Voisin, and Maintenon in a somewhat cavalier fashion. The very idea of saying "no" to a direct order of a minister of war, much less to that of the king, was more than most of the nobility ever dreamed of doing. It is no wonder that the court was shocked by the events of nearly every year. Both Chamillart and Voisin seemed to have been somewhat overawed by Villars. Certainly both men tended to be accommodating to the marshal's fiery personality. Of all the superiors that Villars was reluctantly forced to acknowledge, perhaps Madame de Maintenon had his respect. Since she had aided him in his youth, Villars seemed always ready to listen to her advice when things were the blackest.

What then was Villars' personality? Although he was the foremost general in the declining years of Louis XIV, he was far from being perfect. Personality traits such as impulsiveness (witnessed in decisions at Denain in 1712 and actions at Rastatt in 1714), arrogance (witnessed in the siege of Landau in 1713), and his unwillingness at times to cooperate (witnessed in the 1703 Bavarian campaign) detracted from his military and diplomatic abilities and lessened the trust that Louis XIV might have placed in him. Undeniably they cost Villars the major command within the French army until 1709, when in Flanders there was no one else to send and the king was forced to gamble on his high-strung, erratic marshal. Naturally the king would hesitate to place the main French army in the hands of a man whose virtues of energy, resourcefulness, courage, and loyalty were set against his arrogance, impulsiveness, and unwillingness to cooperate. Personally, however, Louis XIV liked Villars. Perhaps the king saw the dash and colorful vigor that were denied him by the very weight of the system of absolutism. Louis XIV did indeed reward Villars with high military rank and with the prestige and wealth of a dukedom, recognition which was well deserved.

Derived from such a personality, Villars' principle of warfare becomes obvious. It was to find the enemy and to defeat him. Villars was not a theoretician nor a great strategist; there is serious doubt, even, that he was a great tactician such as Gustavus Adolphus or Marshal Saxe. He was essentially a man of action. Though he recognized the importance of mobility, maneuver with him was not a tactical end; instead it was a means whose end was nearly always the decisive encounter. In the encounter itself, his course might be anyone's guess. But several words do seem to outline the type of war that Villars waged, as certain terms describe his personality. These words are audacity, charge when on line, entrenchment, caution, determination, and intimidation. Villars always believed that he could defeat an enemy with far inferior forces if he could feint his adversary into committing a blunder. Yet when an enemy was on the field offering battle, Villars was wont to lead his troops in a headlong charge except when gravely outnumbered and ordered to stand on the defensive. For Villars a defensive position meant elaborate interconnecting field entrenchments with cautious frontal probing to ascertain the enemy's next move. These things—audacity, charge, entrenchment, caution—compose the essence of Villars' battlefield judgment. Rarely was he wrong.

Determination was Villars' word of words. A general simply had at all times to be sure of the eventual success of his army. Certainly Villars' subordinates were convinced that he believed they would win even at times when the marshal was not sure himself. How does a general create this appearance? A haughty air? Willingness to endure hardships? Reputation? Probably the last—reputation—is the correct answer. There could be no doubt that here was a man who had the knack of winning, winning, winning when all the other marshals were losing, losing, losing.

Second only to determination in Villars' vocabulary was the word, intimidation. Here was a real weapon which he constantly employed. Villars was always serious when he threatened to sack a town or to put an entire population to the sword unless capitulation was immediately forthcoming. When the occasion demanded, Villars practiced "total war" as much as did Caesar, Napoleon, and Sherman.

Previous scholarship on Villars has been limited to various writers of memoirs, the opinions of Saint-Simon and the lone biography of Lieutenant Colonel Carré. The extensive comments of the Duke of Saint-Simon and the work of Carré actually form the only real publications on Villars that attempt value judgments. Unfortunately both are polemical in nature. Of the memoirists, the Marquis de Vogüé is the only trustworthy source for what he includes in his various publications. Unfortunately, De Vogüé does not often include materials that cast his ancestor in a bad light. Much additional material, however, is contained in various archives, and many things heretofore undisclosed have been recorded in the previous chapters of this work.

The reason for Villars' disgrace in 1703 and his unyielding atitude in regard to royal orders that he thought incorrect was clear only after close reading of the maze of documents cited in the bibliography. The thinking of Villars on the Camisard uprising, in which he was willing to try any method to end the revolt in order to return to royal favor without having to abase himself, is fully treated for the first time in Chapter 4. His attitudes toward men, material, and conquest are perhaps nowhere else set forth as clearly as in Chapter 5. Other writers have tended to believe Villars the best French general during the declining years of Louis XIV, but they do not give him the credit he is due for the year 1709. It is quite clear that, although

Malplaquet might technically have been an allied victory, the year 1709 saw the door leading to Paris effectively closed. It would not be amiss to say that Villars alone was capable of saving France from military defeat and possible partition after the terrible winter of 1708-1709. Possibly the greatest single characteristic of Villars is brought forth in the campaign of the years 1710-1711, when he was suffering almost constantly with intense pain from his leg wound. Hitherto this wound has been far more interesting as a prime example of battlefield surgery. Past scholarship has paid little attention to the physical and mental agonies of the man that are so clear in his letters home and in his reports to the court. Denain is finally placed in its proper place in history. This battle, or rather skirmish, was the final pressure that forced the Dutch to negotiate at Utrecht, but its true consequence lay in the minds of the imperial princes who began to clamor for an end to the fighting and who gave the Holy Roman Emperor even less support.

The final campaign, which saw Villars take Landau and Freiburg, was really anticlimactic, but it went far to prove that he was not a siege specialist. Only a person who has read his fuming dispatches to the Prince of Württemburg and Baron Harsch can realize his desire for a series of quick decisions and the heartbreak involved when the stubborn resistance of the two fortresses forbade any serious thoughts of penetrating the Empire. The negotiations at Rastatt proved that Villars was not a diplomat. He was not fitted by temperament for the usual slow diplomatic wrangling. What is important is that Villars' drive and determination were effective in the war of the Spanish Succession.

Bibliography

THE GREATEST STORES OF MANUSCRIPT MATERIAL ON THE French side of the War of the Spanish Succession may be found in the rich archives in and around Paris. That on the French Army was found in the Archives de la Guerre. Here countless thousands of dispatches, often less than two hundred words each, were read for the answers concerning Villars in the War of the Spanish Succession. The core of the material on Bourbon France resides in Series A1 (about 4,000 quarto volume of approximately 250 items each). The history of the army of the Old Regime from the mid-sixteenth century is found here. From time to time various archivists and members of the French general staff have added studies and collections of private papers to the archives which are catalogued in Series A2, A3, A4—designated the *Archives administratives, Mémoires historiques,* and *Mémoires techniques.*

When the Archives de la Guerre were separated from the Archives Nationales in 1952, many hundreds of cartons in Series AD6, K, and M for some reason were left behind. These series are of vast importance to any student of French military history. Series AD6 contains what appears to be a complete file of the royal military ordinances from 1546 to 1792, while Series K includes several cartons of correspondence of Louis XIV. Perhaps Series M provided the most fascinating discovery in the Archives Nationales. There are many cartons in this series which contain unclassified materials on the seventeenth and eighteenth century army. Tightly packed into these boxes are thousands of documents which did not fit in specific classifications elsewhere.

The papers found in the Bibliothèque Nationale are, for the purposes of the military historian, in much the same disarray as Series M in the Archives Nationales. The items in the manuscript room of the Bibliothèque Nationale are arranged by number in order of acquisition. My greatest find in this depository was in Register 496 of *Nouveau fonds*. However other items, especially the *Traité de la guerre de campagne* (*Ancien fonds,* Register 6257), provided some insight into Villars' character found nowhere else.

The Archives du Ministère des Affaires Étrangères proved to be the most challenging to me. The printed catalog of this depository provides hardly any information on the character of the documents. Many items have been filed out of order, at times even in the wrong volume. The work of N. L. le Dran, entitled *Histoire de la négociation des traitès de paix conclus aux Congrès de Rastatt et de Bade en 1714 et 1715, pour terminer la Guerre de Succession de l'Espagne* proved to be in the same category with Pelet's *Mémoires militaires.* Le Dran failed to include many of the most important documents readily available in the *Correspondance politique.*

Approximately 1,700 frames of microfilm mostly on the period of January-February 1714 were obtained from the Haus-, Hof-, und Staatsarchiv in Vienna. I hoped to find further evidence of possible collusion between Villars and Eugene in the interests of peace. Unfortunately such information was not found. Perhaps a fuller search of archives in Vienna might reveal the answer to this question.

A general comment is in order concerning the various *Feldzüge* and the *Mémoires militaires.* The *Feldzüge* are the product of an Austrian general staff study of the 1880's. They are well written and narrative in nature. An excellent selection of the correspondence between Prince Eugene and various imperial officials is included as an appendix to each volume. As a rule the various staff officers assigned to this task used whatever printed and archival material of other nations was available to them. Unfortunately, the analytical quality of this set is somewhat maimed by a natural bias and an overemphasis of the actions of Prince Eugene. The *Mémoires militaires* were actually written by the Baron de Vault before 1780 and are taken exclusively from materials located in the Archives de la Guerre. After publication of the long series of *Documents inédits pour l'histoire de France* began in the 1850's, General Pelet, director of the Archives de la Guerre, published the works of De Vault and added supporting documents. This work is biased as might readily be assumed from the author's having free access only to the archival material of one of the major powers involved in the War of the Spanish Succession. In my opinion the Austrian volumes are better works of history.

Two contemporary periodicals are of the utmost importance for this study. The research specialist would do well to check the *Mercure historique et politique* for excellent news stories. This periodical, although published at The Hague, is perfectly trustworthy in its news stories but quite biased in its articles that begin with the word "Réflection." The *Gazette de France* was a semiofficial publication of the French court and must be used with extreme caution. But it is reliable for chronology.

The problem with all the various editions of Villars' *Mémoires* is that they are collections of letters based upon the fragmentary letter books that he left behind. Had Villars been a diarist or note keeper, the task of the biographer would have been far different. Few letters have survived which deal with his private life and his inner thoughts.

In 1736 Guillaume la Pause published three volumes of letters under the title of *Mémoires du duc de Villars*. This work did not have the sanction of the second Duke of Villars nor did the author have entrance to the Royal Archives. La Pause seems to have benefited from a combination of journals, private accounts, published works, and vivid imagination. In the 1780's the descendants of Villars entrusted his files to Louis Pierre Anquetil, who published three volumes, using the title *Vie du maréchal de Villars*. This edition was reproduced several times in the nineteenth century, most notably in the lengthy series of *Mémoires pour servir à l'histoire de France,* Volume IX. Most of the original papers of Villars survived the revolution and eventually came into the hands of the Marquis de Vogüé in 1883. In his six-volume publication of letters and narration entitled *Mémoires du maréchal de Villars,* the marquis stated that the letter books contained material for the periods 1687-1691, 1701-1705, and 1709-1711. These six volumes of the memoirs were followed in 1888 by two additional volumes of correspondence. However, the Marquis de Vogüé located papers in many of the libraries of Europe and included them in his works. The name De Vogüé represents nineteenth-century descendants of Villars. These works are not comprehensive in any sense of the word. It must be said that all three editors were very sympathetic. I believe that all three suppressed information in the cause of their subject. In my possession are many references and letters that were available to both Anquetil and De Vogüé which they either overlooked or ignored.

The general information on the French army included in this work is based upon an exhaustive study of materials contained in the Archives de la Guerre and the Archives Nationales. Especially to be recommended as the most important concentration of primary material on the French army as regards organization, logistics, and other aspects are

AD6, M638, 639, 640, 643, 647, and 649 in the latter and *Mémoires techniques, 1701* and *1715,* in the former. It is surprising how little has been collected and saved concerning the French army during the Old Regime. For instance the papers of the Marquis de Louvois and of Daniel Voisin have never received as exhaustive a treatment as those of personages like the Duc de Saint-Simon. There is every need for a thoughtful, refined study of the Bourbon army, based not only upon the published memoirs and letters but also upon the many thousands of cartons contained in the Archives de la Guerre and the Archives Nationales.

It is this lack of basic documentation that makes almost all the existing secondary studies on the French army lacking in value. Of the printed secondary works only Albert Babeau, *La vie militaire sous l'ancien régime* (Paris, 1890); Louis Etienne Dussieux, *L'armée en France* (Versailles, 1884); Emile G. Léonard, *L'armée et ses problèmes au XVIIIe siècle* (Paris, 1958) ; and Roger S. Quimby, *The Background of Napoleonic Warfare* (New York, 1959), are worthy of consideration. Unfortunately only Léonard's work attempts to discuss the problems of the Bourbon army and even then dwells upon the theme of the army's relationship to contemporary society to the detriment of a detailed discussion of the who's, what's and why's of the military evolution that of necessity must take place within any given society.

Marshal Villars has had only two biographers. The very influential Duc de Saint-Simon's *Mémoires* gave a completely biased opinion of Villars which (after Voltaire's acceptance of them in *Le siècle de Louis XIV*) formed the most influential opinion of Villars in the eighteenth century. This opinion was only partially corrected by the equally biased publications of La Pause, Anquetil and De Vogüé. In 1936 Lieutenant Colonel Henri Carré published *Le Maréchal Villars, homme de guerre et diplomate.* Unfortunately this biography is a polemical treatment even though it does serve as one of two studies on generals of the later years of Louis XIV which have "exploded the idea that Louis had no good generals after Turenne and Condé." (John B. Wolf, *The Emergence of the Great Powers, 1685-1715* [New York, 1951]). Carré based his work on previous publications, only consulting the archival sources on points not covered by the Marquis de Vogüé.

In dealing with the secondary source material, both books and periodicals, I have attempted to list in the bibliography only a minimum of the works consulted.

Manuscript Materials

FOR AUSTRIA

Acten des K. u. K. Haus-, Hof-, und Staatsarchiv, "Rastatter Freiden." Volumes 174b, 175: January and February 1714.

FOR FRANCE

Archives de la Guerre:

A. Series A1. Registers 1465, 1568-1573, 1582, 1596, 1616, 1617, 1639, 1675-1677, 1712, 1715, 1716, 1796-1799, 1851-1853, 1845-1848, 1948-1953, 2027, 2028, 2030, 2091, 2099-2101, 2108, 2149-2152, 2154, 2213-2217, 2224, 2299, 2302-2306, 2308, 2374-2386, 2387, 2388, 2422, 2453-2461, 2470, 1487, 2506.

B. Series A2. Carton 11: Several memoirs covering the 1700-1714 period.

C. Series A4. Cartons 4: Flanders, Germany, Italy, 1695-1705; 5: Flanders, Germany, Italy, 1702-1704; 7: Flanders, Germany, 1701-1709; 8: Correspondence of the duc du Maine; 9: Germany, 1713-1715.

D. *Archives administratives.* 174: Personnel file on Villars.

E. *Mémoires historiques.* 72: A file of copies of documents and reports relating to the battle of Malplaquet in the archives of Berlin, Copenhagen, The Hague, Marburg, Munich, and the libraries of Strasbourg and Stuttgart; 79-92: Extracts of the correspondence of the court and the generals during the War of the Spanish Succession—Germany, 1701-1713; 93: Unsigned account of the siege of Freiburg in 1713; 94-118: Extracts of the correspondence of the court and the generals during the War of the Spanish Succession—Italy, 1701-1712; 115: Account of the conquests of the duc de Savoie in the campaign of 1708 by Louis André Guiber; 124: Accounts of various expeditions during the War of the Spanish Succession:

(a) Particulars of the battle of Friedlingen, (b) Camp of Sierck, (c) Details of the operations beyond the Rhine in 1707, (d) Notes on the campaign in Germany in 1707, (e) Detail of the siege of Fenestrelles in 1708;

126. Flanders, 1559-1713:

(a) Notes on the campaign of 1709, (b) Several unsigned accounts of the battle of Malplaquet, (c) The siege of Douai in 1710, (d) Notes on the campaign of 1712, (e) Projects and notes relative to the sieges of Bouchain, Douai, and Landrecies in 1712;

58-70: Extracts of the correspondence of the court and the generals during the War of the Spanish Succession—Flanders, 1701-1713.

F. *Mémoires techniques.* 1701: Infantry memoirs, 1589-1732; 1725: Cavalry memoirs, 1646-1790.

Archives de la Ministère des Affaires Étrangères:
A. *Correspondance politique*—Austria. 92-100: January 1713-December 1714.
B. Memoirs. 56-57: N. L. le Dran, *Histoire de la négociation des traités de paix conclus aux congrès de Rastadt et Bade en 1714 et 1715, pour terminer la guerre de succession Espagne.*

Archives Nationales:
A. Series AD6. Cartons 1: Artillery, 1546-1780; 2: Cavalry, 1688-1788; 4: Commissioners of War, 1523-1788, composition and organization of the army, 1523-1788; 5: Leave; 9: Discipline, 1575-1788; 10: Rights and privileges, 1674-1789; 14, 15: Militia, 1559-1763; 16: Powders and saltpetres, 1540-1750; 17: Prisoners of war and recruitment, 1649-1780; 18: Pay.
B. Series K. Cartons 121a: Correspondence of Louis XIV, 1686-1711; 121b: Correspondence of Louis XIV, 1693-1710; 122-135: Correspondence of Louis XIV, 1707-1714 (one carton).
C. Series M. Cartons 638-640, 643, 647, 659: Mixtures, wars, XVII-XVIII centuries.

Bibliothèque de l'Arsenal. Registers 5770: Parlement of Grenoble, 1706; 6624: Letters of Villars to Du Bourg, 1705-1706.

Bibliothèque de Sainte-Geneviève. Register 2100, Folio 1: Documents relative to the memoirs of Villars.

Bibliothèque Nationale:

A. Ancien fonds. Registers 6257: *Traité de la guerre de campagne,* by Villars; 8959: Letters of Villars to Lebret, intendant of Provence, 1712-1728; 9716: *Mémoires instructifs contenant l'état de l'Europe avant le traité de Riswick, et tout ce qui c'est passé de plus remarquable, tant à la cour que dans les opérations de la guerre jusqu'en l'année 1710, sous M. le maréchal de Villars,* M. le marquis de Fequières, lt. gen. of the armies of the king, 1710; 10233: File of memoirs on the War of the Spanish Succession, 1700-1714; 20625: Pieces on the history of France—Folios 417[27], Maréchal de Boufflers, 417[30], Voisin; 20865, Folio 333: Letter of Villars to Counte de Lyonne; 20866, Folio 209: Copies concerning the history of France, War of the Spanish Succession, letters on military operations.

B. Nouveau fonds. Registers 496: Letters of Villars to Max Emmanuel, 1702-1703; 498: Correspondence of Du Bourg and Voisin; 3155: Various military memoirs.

Primary Printed Source Materials

Aigaliers, Jacques Jacob de Kassel, baron d'. *Mémoires et lettres.* Paris, 1935.

Anquetil, Louis Pierre, *vie du maréchal duc de Villars.* 3 vols. Paris, 1787.

Boislisle, A. M. de. *Correspondance des contrôleurs-généraux des finances avec les intendants des provinces.* Vols. II and III. Paris, 1883.

Catinat, Nicolas. *Mémoires et correspondance.* Edited by M. Bernard. Paris, 1819.

Coxe, William. *Memoirs of John Duke of Marlborough with his Original Correspondence.* Vol. I. London, 1818.

Dangeau, Philippe de Courcillon, duc de. *Journal.* Edited by Feuillet de Conches. Vols. VIII-XV. Paris, 1854-1860.

Danzer, Alphons. *Spanischer Successions-Krieg, Feldzug 1703.* Vienna, 1878.

Dumont, Edmond. *Histoire militaire du Prince Eugène*. The Hague, 1729.

Eberswald, Heinrich Siegler Edlen von. *Spanischer Successions-Krieg, Feldzug 1712*. Vienna, 1887.

Fénelon, François de Salignac de la Mothe. *Oeuvres complètes de Fénelon*. Edited by Jean-Joseph Bénichet. 19 vols. Toulouse, 1810.

Grünbühl, Emil Freiherrn Mayerhofer von, and Camille Freiherrn Komers von Lindenbach. *Spanischer Successions-Krieg, Feldzug 1706*. Vienna, 1882.

Hipssich, Carl Freiherrn von. *Spanischer Successions-Krieg, Feldzug 1710*. Vienna, 1887.

——————, and Camille Freiherrn Komers von Lindenbach. *Spanischer Successions-Krieg, Feldzug 1707*. Vienna, 1883.

Isambert, François André, and others. *Recueil général des anciennes lois françaises depuis l'an 420 jusqu'à la révolution de 1789*. Vols. XIX-XX. Paris, 1831-1833.

Kirckhammer, Alexander. *Spanischer Successions-Krieg, Feldzug 1708*. Vienna, 1885.

Machalicky, Ottokar. *Spanischer Successions-Krieg, Feldzug 1713*. Vienna, 1892.

Maintenon, Françoise d'Aubigné, Marquise de. *Lettres*. Vol. VII. Amsterdam, 1756.

Mühliverth-Gartner, Friedrich Freiherrn. *Spanischer Successions-Krieg, Feldzug 1711*. Vienna, 1887.

Murray, George (ed.). *The Letters and Dispatches of John Churchill . . . from 1702-1712*. Vols. I-II, IV-V. London, 1845.

Parke, Gilbert. *Letters and Correspondence of Henry Saint-John. . . .* Vol. II. London, 1798.

Pelet, Louis. *Mémoires militaires relatifs à la succession d'Espagne sous Louis XIV, extraits de la cour et des généraux. . . .* 11 vols. Paris, 1862.

Plantavit la Pause, Guillaume, abbé de Margon. *Mémoires du duc de Villars. . . .* The Hague, 1758.

Quincy, Joseph Sevin, comte de. *Mémoires*. Edited by Leon Lecestre. Vol. I. Paris, 1901.

Rechberger, Josef Ritter. *Spanischer Successions-Krieg, Feldzug 1709*. Vienna, 1886.

Rechkorn, Josef Rechberger Ritter von. *Spanischer Successions-Krieg, Feldzug 1705*. Vienna, 1881.

Saint-Simon, Louis de Rouvroy, duc de. *Mémoires*. Edited by A. M. de Boislisle and L. Lecestre. 41 vols. Paris, 1879-1928.

Vic, Claude de, and J. Vaisette. *Histoire générale de Languedoc.* Edited by Édouard Dulaurier and others. Vols. XII-XIV. Toulouse, 1872-1892.

Vogüé, Charles Jean Melchoir, marquis de. *Madame de Maintenon et le maréchal de Villars, correspondance inédite.* Paris, 1856.

——————. *Mémoires du duc de Villars.* 6 vols. Paris, 1884-1906.

——————. *Villars, d'après sa correspondance.* . . . 2 vols. Paris, 1888.

Voltaire, François Marie Arouet de. *Le siècle de Louis XIV.* Leipzig, 1754.

Wetzer, Leander Heinrich. *Spanischer Successions-Krieg, Feldzug 1701.* Vienna, 1876.

——————. *Spanischer Successions-Krieg, Feldzug 1702.* Vienna, 1887.

Vauban, Sébastien le Prestre, marquis de. *A Project for a Royal Tythe.* London, 1708.

Secondary Printed Materials

Alison, Archibald. *The Life of John Duke of Marlborough.* Vol. II. London, 1855.

Almeras, Charles. *La Révolte des Camisards.* Paris, 1960.

Anderson, Matthew S. *Europe in the Eighteenth Century.* New York, 1961.

Andréadès, A. *History of the Bank of England.* London, 1909.

Arneth, Alfred R. von. *Prinz Eugen von Savonen.* Vol. II. Vienna, 1864.

Ashley, Maurice P. *Marlborough.* London, 1939.

Atkenson, C. T. *Marlborough and the Rise of the British Army.* New York, 1941.

Babeau, Albert. *La vie militaire sous l'ancien régime.* 2 vols. Paris, 1890.

Baird, Henry M. *The Huguenots and the Revocation of the Edict of Nantes.* New York, 1895.

Bray, Anna E. *The Revolt of the Protestants of the Cévennes.* London, 1870.

Cabanès, Docteur [Auguste]. *Chirurgiens et blessés à travers l'histoire.* . . . Paris, 1918.

Carré, Henri. *Maréchal de Villars.* . . . Paris, 1936.

Carsten, F. L. (ed.). *The Ascendancy of France, 1648-1688*. Vol. V, *The New Cambridge Modern History*. Cambridge, 1961.

Cavalier, Jean. *Memoirs of the Wars of the Cévennes*. London, 1727.

Churchill, Winston S. *Marlborough*. . . . 6 vols. New York, 1933-1938.

Court, Antoine. *Histoire des troubles de Cévennes*. Ville-franche, 1760.

Dedieu, Joseph. *Le rôle politique des Protestants français*. Paris, 1920.

Ducasse, André. *La guerre des Camisards*. Paris, 1946.

Dussieux, Louis Etienne. *L'armée en France*. Vol. II. Versailles, 1884.

Fortesque, John W. *History of the British Army*. Vol. I. London, 1889.

————. *Marlborough*. London, 1932.

Grubb, Arthur P. *Jean Cavalier*. . . . London, 1931.

Issarte, Abel. *Des causes de la révolte des Camisards*. Montbéliard, 1901.

La Baume, Charles de. *Relation historique de la révolte des fanatiques ou des Camisards*. Nîmes, 1874.

La Gorce, Agnès de. *La guerre des Camisards*. Paris, 1950.

Lavisse, Ernest, and Alfred Rambaud, *Historie générale du IVe siècle à nos jours*. Vol. VI. Paris, 1895.

Léonard, Emile G. *L'armée et ses problèmes au XVIIIe siècle*. Paris, 1958.

Mignet, François-Auguste-Alexis. *Négociations relatives à la succession d'Espagne sous Louis XIV*. 4 vols. Paris, 1835-1842.

Moret, Ernest, *Quinze ans du règne de Louis XIV*. 3 vols. Paris, 1859.

Nussbaum, Frederick L. *The Triumph of Science and Reason, 1660-1685*. New York, 1953.

Pin, Marcel. *Jean Cavalier*. Nîmes, 1936.

Preston, Richard A., and others. *Men in Arms*. New York, 1956.

Quimby, Roger S. *The Background of Napoleonic Warfare*. New York, 1959.

Saint-Leger, Albert, and Philip Sagnac. *La préponderance française*. Paris, 1935.

Sautai, Maurice. *La manoeuvre de Denain*. Lille, 1902.

Stanhope, Philip. *History of England Comprising the Reign of Queen Anne until the Peace of Utrecht*. London, 1870.

Taylor, Frank. *The Wars of Marlborough, 1702-1709*. Oxford, 1921.
Trevelyan, George. *England Under Queen Anne*. 3 vols. London, 1934.
Vogüé, Charles Jean Melchoir, marquis de. *Villars et l'électeur de Bavière*. Paris, 1885.
Wolf, John B. *The Emergence of the Great Powers, 1685-1715*. New York, 1951.

Periodicals

"Bâville to Chamillart." *Bulletin de la Société de l'histoire du Protestantisme française*, XXIV (1876), 136.
Duvivier, Georges. "La guerre de la succession d'Espagne," *Journal des sciences militaires*, IX-XII (1827-1828).
Gazette de France, 1700-1714.
Mercure historique et politique, 1701-1714.
Paux, Frank. "Origines, causes, et conséquences de la guerre des Camisards," *Revue historique*, CXXIX (September-December 1819), 1-21.

Bibliographical Aids

Akademie der Wissenschaften. *Allgemeine Deutsche Biographie*. Leipzig, 1879.
André, Louis, and others. *Les sources de l'histoire de France*. Vols. V and VII. Paris, 1926.
Böhm, Bruno. *Bibliographie zur Geschichte des Prinzen Eugen von Savoyen und seiner Zeit*. Vienna, 1943.
Dictionnaire de la noblesse. Paris, 1772.
Hoefer, J. F. C. *Nouvelle biographie générale depuis les temps les plus réculés jusqu'à nos jours*. Paris, 1852-1866.
Internationale Bibliographie de Zeitschriftenliterature. Bibliographie der Deutschen Zeitschriftenliterature, 1876-1962. Bibliographic der Fremdsprachigen Zeitschriftenliterature, 1911-1962. Osnabrück, various years.
Kohler, Charles. *Catalogue des manuscripts de la Bibliothèque Mazarin*. Paris, 1896.
Martin, Henry. *Catalogue des manuscripts de la Bibliothèque de L'Arsenal*. Paris, 1896.

Ministère de la Guerre. *Inventaire-sommaire des archives historiques*. Paris, 1896.

―――――. *Archives de la Guerre*. By Louis Tuetey. Paris, 1896.

Ministère de l'Education Nationale. *Catalogue général des manuscripts français*. Paris, 1895.

―――――. *Catalogue général des livres imprimès de la Bibliothèque Nationale*. Paris, 1931-1962.

―――――. *Catalogue de l'histoire de France*. Paris, 1855. Supplemental volume: *Histoire militaire et maritime,* 1894.

Ministère des Affaires Étrangères. *État sommaire des archives du départment des affaires étrangères*. By Pierre Deluns-Montord and others. Vol. I. Paris, 1903.

―――――. *État numérique des fonds de la correspondance politique de l'origine à 1871*. By Abel Kigault and others. Paris, 1936.

Index

ABOUT THE AUTHOR

CLAUDE C. STURGILL, a native of Floyd County, Kentucky, holds the Ph.D. degree in history from the University of Kentucky, where he also completed his undergraduate work. The academic year 1961-1962 he spent in Paris, doing research in French archives and libraries for his dissertation, of which this book is a revision. He has taught at the University of Kentucky and at Western Kentucky State College; he is presently assistant professor of European history at Wisconsin State University, Oshkosh.

ABOUT THE BOOK

MARSHAL VILLARS AND THE WAR OF THE SPANISH SUCCESSION was composed and printed in the Printing Department of the University of Kentucky. It is set in Linotype Baskerville, with headings in ATF Bernhard Modern. The typographic design and the jacket artwork are by Elaine Sherer. The book is printed on Warren Olde Style antique wove stock and bound by the C. J. Krehbiel Company, Cincinnati, in Columbia Bayside Linen cloth.